when

HEAVEN

invades

EARTH

for teens

DESTINY IMAGE BOOKS BY BILL JOHNSON

A Life of Miracles

Dreaming with God

Face to Face

Release the Power of Jesus

Strengthen Yourself in the Lord

The Supernatural Power of a Transformed Mind

When Heaven Invades Earth

when

HEAVEN

invades

EARTH

for teens

YOUR GUIDE TO
GOD'S SUPERNATURAL POWER

Bill Johnson
and Michael Seth

DESTINY IMAGE® PUBLISHERS, INC.

P.O. Box 310, Shippensburg, PA 17257-0310

"Promoting Inspired Lives."

Previously published as Here Comes Heaven by Destiny Image
Previous ISBN: 978-0768425024

This book and all other Destiny Image, Revival Press, MercyPlace, Fresh Bread, Destiny Image Fiction, and Treasure House books are available at Christian bookstores and distributors worldwide.

For a U.S. bookstore nearest you, call 1-800-722-6774.

For more information on foreign distributors, call 717-532-3040.

Reach us on the Internet: www.destinyimage.com.

ISBN 13 TP: 978-0-7684-4253-3

ISBN 13 Ebook: 978-0-7684-8455-7

For Worldwide Distribution, Printed in the U.S.A.

1 2 3 4 5 6 7 8 / 18 17 16 15 14

DEDICATIONS

To those who see children through the Father's eyes.

MIKE SETH

I dedicate this book to my grandchildren—Kennedy and Selah, Haley and Tea, Judah and Diego, and the two that are on the way—Braden and Isabella. May you always enjoy the adventure of bringing His world into ours.

BILL JOHNSON

ACKNOWLEDGMENTS

Bill Johnson—a true father who gave me an invitation to pursue my destiny and live a dream.

Bethel Church—an "open heaven" where advancing the Kingdom is not just an idea, but a reality.

Marilyn—Thank you for your support, encouragement, and ideas. You are a wonderful source of strength. I love you.

CONTENTS

PART I

HERE COMES HEAVEN

Chapter 1

HEAVEN ON EARTH

Bungoma kids for Jesus! Bungoma kids for Jesus!" The cry was filling the city of Bungoma, in the country of Kenya in Africa. The streets were packed with over 2,000 kids singing, dancing, marching, and carrying signs proclaiming, "Bungoma belongs to Jesus!"

Something huge was happening. Heaven opened up, and God's presence was just raining down on the town, with miracles invading everywhere. Hospitals, prisons, businesses, churches—it was all changing. The most amazing thing was that God was using His kids to bring Heaven to earth!

How did this happen? Just one year ago, Bungoma was very different. Many of the pastors didn't think that God would ever use kids to show off His power. They even thought you couldn't get saved until you were an adult!

God wasn't having any more of that. The Lord began to speak to the leaders about His kids. God wanted young people to be seen and respected as valuable treasures. He wanted them shining in His presence, love, and power. God had plans to use the youth in a mighty way. The leaders listened to God's instructions and invited youth ministers to Bungoma. They gathered kids from the churches, orphanages, and streets and began telling them about Jesus.

As these kids felt the Father's love and believed His words, they began to move in the power of God, and miracles started cropping up everywhere. One group of kids went to a hospital. The leaders said, "Okay. Just listen to the Lord, and do whatever Jesus says to do." The people in the hospital were sad, hurting, and sick—and not exactly thrilled to have visitors.

The kids started praying, and one boy said, "I feel like God wants me to sing." So he just raised his hands and sang a worship song right there, and as he sang, God's presence filled the room. The sick people suddenly felt the touch of God and began to cry, starving for more of Him. They asked the kids to come and show them how to receive Jesus. It was an awesome day!

After that, the kids wanted to do a whole lot more, working together with God. They didn't want to wait until they were grown up when God could use them right now!

The kids went out and started praying for the entire city. People met the Lord and their bodies were healed. More and more kids and teenagers got together, and soon there were prayer meetings taking place all over the city as the youth prayed for God to do great things in Bungoma. That's when God gave them a plan.

The Plan

In Bungoma, leaders in different churches did not hang out with each other—they just stuck to their own church and hung out with "their people." But the kids didn't care. They were all friends who prayed together. They decided to just serve the city's pastors. The leaders were amazed and touched. They ended up apologizing for ignoring the youth and acting like religious cliques. The adults began to catch on as God brought the churches together, with the kids leading the way!

God told the youth to march for seven days and have special meetings throughout the city. The day before they began to march, the pastors came and asked their forgiveness for not valuing them as people who could know God and do powerful miracles with Him. They prayed over the kids and teenagers and gave them a large key, symbolizing how the leaders honored them for carrying God's power and authority and doing great things!

For the next seven days, the kids marched and shared God's love and power all over the city. People were saved and healed, and they saw tons of amazing miracles. In one hospital, over 100 people were healed in a single day—they were sent home in perfect health! A few weeks later in another hospital, the kids were praying for people to be healed. God answered them by healing so many people—before they could even be treated at the hospital—that the hospital had to close down! Today that building is being used for business offices. Nobody needs a hospital there anymore!

Every day, the kids took the lead in special meetings. It was powerful! They preached, led worship, and touched people with God's power. Pastors were starting to get an idea of just how important and powerful young people are, and how much God wanted to shake the world through them.

What happened during that seven-day march in August of 2002 was just the beginning. Young people from other parts of Kenya started doing the same things. Now, all over the nation of Kenya people are asking kids to come and minister to them. In Bungoma, the kids still go to the orphanages, hand out food and clothes, and minister in the villages and hospitals. School teachers and principals, businessmen and women, government officials, and even leaders in other religions have come together to honor and bless what these kids have accomplished. Pastors in the area have also joined forces to help the street children. Orphans who used to wander the streets are being adopted into Christian homes where they have a family, food, clothing, and a place to learn about God.

You better believe that kids are priceless in Bungoma now! People finally got the message—God loves them and thinks they're amazing! He sees His kids as mighty and powerful— warriors for Him who bring Heaven and the Kingdom of God to earth!

Jennifer Toledo told us this amazing story. She was a big part of training and leading the kids who transformed Bungoma, Kenya.

Jesus Loves the Youth

What a crazy awesome story! Just think—kids and teenagers, full of God's power, changed an entire city! If you've never heard a story like this before, guess what? This stuff is normal in God's eyes! Living in God's radical love and doing powerful things, like performing miracles, is totally, 100 percent normal.

When people find out who their Father is and how much He loves them—they become powerful! When they discover that His power and authority can be theirs, they start working miracles. Kids and teenagers just like you can catch hold of Heaven!

You might be thinking, "Yeah, but that was in Africa. Things are different there." Well, God isn't different there, is He? God wants His kids all over the world to radiate with His power, love, and glory. You can show others just what He can do! God loves you—you are His special treasure. And you can do mighty and powerful things for Him right now. God will use you to change the world!

I'm inviting you on a journey. This is going to be an adventure—it starts now, and it'll continue for the rest of your life!

Your heavenly Father has a lot to show you about who He is, how much He loves you, who you are, and what you get to do for Him. God has some things to give you for this journey—your own personal adventure. Let's bring Heaven to earth!

Chapter 2

A ROYAL MISSION

Did you know Jesus couldn't heal the sick? He couldn't help people who were demon-possessed either. You might say, "No way! Jesus did all those things. It's in the Bible."

But look what Jesus said about Himself in John 5:19—"I can do nothing." That means He didn't bring any special powers with Him when He came to earth. Even though Jesus was 100 percent God, He chose to live on earth as a regular person just like you. Why would He do that?

Because He loves you.

Jesus did many miracles, and He did them *as a person,* a human being who was very close to His heavenly Father. If Jesus did all those miracles as God, then you couldn't do them, because you're human. But because Jesus healed the sick, raised the dead, and cast out demons *as a person—you can too!*

So if Jesus was a human being, what was so special about Him?

Well, He had no sin, so He was as close as possible to His heavenly Father.

He knew He needed some help.

He needed the awesome power of God—the Holy Spirit.

How about you?

If you have Jesus in your heart, your sins are already forgiven. You are already close to God, your heavenly Dad. When Jesus died on the Cross, He destroyed the power of sin—*forever!* His blood has washed you and made your heart clean. When God looks at you, He actually sees His Son, Jesus. Nothing can keep you away from your heavenly Father— *nothing!*

*And...*you can have God's miraculous, awesome power in your life.

The Battle

God had a plan for His Kingdom to cover the earth, but He had an enemy who was out to stop Him.

Lucifer was the most gorgeous angel God ever made. He was Heaven's worship leader—and the worship in Heaven is intense! The Bible says that thousands of angels and other creatures worship before God's throne nonstop. It sounds like a roaring waterfall—and they don't even use a sound system. (Read Revelation 19:6.) The worship in Heaven makes the loudest concert on earth sound lame and boring!

Lucifer was leading this heavenly concert of praise—he was right up at the front, looking his best and doing a great job...until it happened. Pride. Lucifer saw God getting all the adoration, even though lucifer himself was so beautiful and such an amazing leader. All full of himself, lucifer decided that all of Heaven should be worshiping *him* instead of God—so he would just have to take God's place on the throne. He pulled together one third of the angels in Heaven, and they went to war against God. As humans, we probably can't even imagine what that was like. It was the most epic battle ever fought.

But it was two against one from the start, and besides that, they were fighting against God Himself. What was lucifer thinking? They never had a chance! He and his angels were hurled out of Heaven and banished to earth, where they roam to this day. Lucifer's name became satan, and the angels who foolishly followed him became demons.

Really, God could have destroyed the devil and his demons without even breaking a sweat, but He chose to defeat darkness in the earth another way.

The Master Plan

When God created Adam and Eve, He put them in an incredible place, custom-made just for them—the Garden of Eden. There was no pain, sickness, or suffering in the Garden. No danger, no misery. It was full of joy, beauty, peace, and God Himself. It was a literal Heaven on earth.

The first man and woman were made in God's image. They could have fun with God, enjoy His love, and love Him back. Plus, Adam and Eve each had their own immortal spirits. They were going to live with God forever. Being made in God's image also meant that they had authority on earth. God gave them the power to rule over the earth He had made for them. He put them in charge of it all, and then gave Adam and Eve a job—have kids who would love Him. As a family, they would spread the heavenly Father's Kingdom of joy and peace all over the earth.

Lost Keys

Satan saw all this going on, and pretty soon he wanted what Adam and Eve had—the "keys" of power and authority. If he could just get those keys, he could make himself king of the earth, and everybody would have to worship him. But how could he pull this off? Since losing the war in Heaven, he had no power. He couldn't invade the Garden of Eden and just take the keys. So the evil prince, satan, had to come up with a plan to trick Adam and Eve.

Satan disguised himself as a snake. He found Eve by the Tree of the Knowledge of Good and Evil. Of course, satan knew that God had told Adam and Eve not to eat this tree's fruit. God didn't want them to know what evil was really like—He wanted them to live in the paradise of love He'd made for them, without anything ruining their relationship. But satan lied to Eve. He twisted God's words and convinced her that she could be like God and know everything if she ate the fruit from the tree.

Tragically, Eve believed the snake's lie. She and Adam agreed with the devil and disobeyed God. The second they ate the fruit, it was done! They gave away the keys of authority to the enemy. The devil now had the power to steal, kill, and destroy all of God's perfect creation.

Sadly, it was Adam and Eve's choice to rebel against God—they made the decision, and now they had to pay the price. They became slaves to sin when they should have been rulers over the whole earth. They couldn't spread God's Kingdom of love and goodness—they were under the authority and power of the devil, who hated them. Sin came in and separated them from their Father, who loved them.

It was the worst day in history.

Rescue!

But God wasn't done with us yet. He knew what to do—He would send us His Son, Jesus. Jesus would take the punishment for Adam and Eve's sin. He would take back what they lost—the keys of power and authority. God the Father not only loved His Son, He loved His humans. He loves you. He was willing to let His own Son die so that everyone could come to Him and enjoy His massive amounts of love. It was the Father's master plan.

Obviously, satan was not okay with this.

Jesus showed up on planet Earth as a human, He got baptized in water and in the Holy Spirit, and then He headed for the desert. The plan was to spend time with His Father, listen to His voice, and get ready for His ministry.

That's when satan came to tempt Jesus. He said, "If You just bow down and worship me, I'll give You those keys You want" (Matt. 4:9, paraphrased). If Jesus would worship satan, even for a second, then He would not have to die on the Cross.

But Jesus knew what God was planning. He knew He was here on earth to suffer and die to get the keys back. Satan's idea might have sounded tempting, but Jesus said, "No!" (see Matt. 4:10). He wouldn't be tempted—He would do this right, and obey and honor His Father. He wasn't going to play satan's game.

See, Father God planned for satan to be defeated by someone who was made in God's own image—Jesus. Jesus would suffer a horrible death in order to bring people back to God. When Jesus died on the Cross and was raised from the dead, satan was totally beaten. Jesus won, and He took back the keys of power and authority over the whole earth. Right now, He's the one in charge. The devil is nothing but a loser!

You Were Born to Rule

When you asked Jesus into your heart, you were totally forgiven for all your sins. But you get even more than that! Jesus has decided to share the reward for His victory over sin and death. That's right—He shares the keys of power and authority with *you!*

You were born to be a ruler here on earth! You are a royal son or daughter of the King of the universe. Jesus said, "All authority has been given to Me in Heaven and earth, and now it's all yours!" (Read Matthew 28:18.) The Father still wants people to rule this planet and spread His Kingdom, and this master plan now includes you. In the world's system, you have to wait until you're old enough before you can get your driver's license or vote, but in God's Kingdom there are no age limits. You are a Royal Ruler right *now!*

So here's how things stand in your domain—even though satan lost the keys and has no power, sin is still running around in the world. It's like bad acne that just won't go away, popping up all over the place and ruining what God made to be perfect. Disease, sickness, poverty, fear, wars, and hate are all here on earth because of sin. Being a Royal Ruler means you get to find and destroy these pimples of evil. Satan has the human race in chains, and we have to break them free. That rotten devil is *still* jealous of God, but there is just no way he can kick God off His throne. The only thing he can do now is hurt the people God loves so dearly.

God has a few things to share with you, as His Royal Ruler on earth—a couple heavenly treasures to spread around in His Kingdom—His peace and goodness, His promises and love. You also have the power and authority to share these treasures with others, and this stuff can seriously change people's lives. Sickness, fear, and all the evil things the devil throws at people will be smashed to bits and disappear. Amazing things will happen!

An Invitation

This is going to be an awesome journey. You are about to find out what it means to be a prince or princess in your Father's heavenly court. You literally have *no idea* how special and valuable you are.

You have a critical mission—spread the Kingdom of God wherever you go, and bring Heaven to earth. All the Father wants is for you to love Him and be close to Him, just like Jesus was when He was on earth.

Time with Your King

As you come into God's presence, begin to think about what Jesus did for you.

He died on the Cross, and you have been forgiven of your sin.

Nothing can stop Him from loving you. Nothing can take you away from His presence. Praise and thank Him for that.

Ask the Father to give you a picture of what He sees when He looks at you.

You are a Prince or Princess. Take a look at the keys.

Ask God to show you what your royal mission is. He will be with you every step of the way.

Journal Time

1. What did God tell you He sees when He looks at you?

2. What did He show you about your Royal Mission?

3. Do you think you can do the same things Jesus did while He was on earth?

Mission Objectives

Ask God to show you how you can give away your "treasures" to others.

Look for people who need God's kindness, peace, and love.

Ask someone who is sick if you can pray for them. Write down what happened.

Chapter 3

TURN AROUND AND SEE

Jesus was always shocking people. Everyone thought He would come to earth as a rich king who would totally eliminate all evil. People expected Him to lead a massive army and take over the world. They thought He would take out their enemies for good. Instead, He came as a little baby—surprise!

They were right about one thing, though—Jesus did come to destroy their enemy. It just wasn't the human enemy they thought He'd be after. Jesus was more interested in destroying sin, the devil, and his reign of terror. But He had to do it according to God's plan.

While most people were busy being shocked and getting offended with Jesus, there were a select few who welcomed Him. These people were lonely for God. They had grown up hearing stories about a coming savior, so when Jesus came, they believed. They didn't care if He wasn't hanging out in a throne room like a king. They were still willing to give up everything to follow Him—their Savior, their Healer, the One who would give them life

When Jesus said, "The Kingdom of Heaven is at hand" (read Matt. 4:17), these people were ready for the party! They knew Jesus wasn't just some poor baby born in a barn. He brought the Kingdom of Heaven with Him!

A Treasure Hunt

When I was a kid, my friends and I played a game called "treasure hunt." Someone would hide the "treasure," usually a stick or a ball, out in a field. Then they would yell, "Search!" The rest of us would begin to look for the treasure—backward. It's pretty hard to look for something while walking backward, but that was the challenge. Sometimes the treasure would be right behind me—I was seconds away from winning, but I had no idea. I could have won instantly if it wasn't against the rules to turn around.

In the same way, our treasure—God's Kingdom—is right here on earth beside us. If you're looking around for God's Kingdom and you don't see it, don't worry. It's invisible—for now. Jesus called out to His listeners, "Repent! Because the Kingdom of Heaven is right here. It's right by your hand" (Matt. 4:17 paraphrased). *Repent* means *stop walking backward and turn around!*

To *repent* actually means to change the way you think about things—things like who God is and what He wants to do here on earth. When you begin to change your thoughts and ask your heavenly Father to come and show you His love, God gives you a whole new way of seeing! Call them "faith eyes." They'll let you see the invisible world. Sounds like a comic book mutant power, doesn't it? But it's a real thing, and Jesus Himself had this Kingdom x-ray vision—it's called *faith*, and you can have it too!

When you can activate your x-ray faith and see God's Kingdom, you'll *feel* just how close God really is. Your heavenly Father will show you things you can't see with regular old eyesight, like God's power to heal. It is more real and powerful than "seeing" a sick person and knowing what's wrong with them. You will get a look at things in God's world, stuff straight out of Heaven—like His never-ending peace, love, goodness, and kindness. Pretty soon, you'll be able to see just how short-lived things like fighting, misery, and anger are. These worldly things don't last a minute compared to Heaven and the love of God!

Hide and Seek

When my sons were little, one of their favorite Easter traditions was the Easter egg hunt. My job was to hide the eggs. I had to put them in places that the boys could go—no eggs on the roof of the house, sadly—but still make sure my kids would have to really search to find them. As they searched, I would walk with them and make sure they didn't miss any eggs. Sometimes I had to give them a few hints, but I was just as happy and excited as they were every time they found an egg.

I was hiding those so my sons *could* find them, and God does the same thing with some of the really cool stuff in His Kingdom. In Proverbs it says, "It is God's privilege to conceal things and the king's privilege to discover them" (Prov. 25:2). That doesn't mean your Father wants to keep His Kingdom a secret—far from it. It's just that some things work better for someone who desperately wants to know God. If you have a hungry heart for Him, your faith will let you see God and His world—including those treasures He hid for you. Your Dad in Heaven gets pumped when you put in the effort and end up discovering awesome treasures about Him and His Kingdom! He's so into this treasure hunt, He'll even help you!

The King's Kingdom

In any kingdom, the people need a good king. When all the decisions for the country are made by one person, you better hope that this ruler is interested in helping his people live safe and happy lives, rather than just making himself rich! If you have a bad king, life can get really hard, really quick. If you have a good king, life works out a lot better for everyone.

Jesus qualifies as pretty much the best King ever. He came to earth to give away Heaven's best stuff to anyone who would obey Him and join His Kingdom. What are those good things? Jesus forgave sinners, miraculously healed the sick, and set people free from everything the devil had been torturing them with—those are some pretty good things!

If we put this as plain and simple as we can, God's Kingdom equals everything in Heaven coming right down here to earth. And Heaven isn't just a bunch of angels sitting on fluffy white clouds playing harps! Nope! We're talking about a place full of wild joy, health and strength, peace, and unbeatable love. That is why Jesus wants us to pray, "May your Kingdom come soon. May your will be done on earth, as it is in heaven" (Matt. 6:10). God's mission is to give you Heaven's best things to enjoy and spread around everywhere you go.

Jesus' Greatest Message

While Jesus was on earth preaching and working miracles, He was the number-one hot topic in Israel. Forget camping out all night for tickets—these people would walk for *days* just to see Jesus heal and to hear Him teach. They brought Him people who were sick—even the incurable ones. They brought people who were so demon-possessed that they were screaming lunatics and no one could help them. And they brought people who had birth defect—those who had been born blind, born deaf, or never walked before in their lives. They came to Jesus, and He healed *all* of them! Not just half of them; not even most of them—*all!* One hundred percent success! We can't even count how many people He healed and set free. (Check out John 21:25.)

After doing all these miracles, Jesus started teaching. He gave a message called the Sermon on the Mount, which started, "God blesses those who are poor and realize their need for Him, for the Kingdom of Heaven is theirs" (Matt. 5:3). Thousands of people were sitting along the hillside, eager to hear what this amazing man had to say. Jesus could see straight into the hearts of the people. They had walked for days, leaving all their stuff behind, *just to be with Him.* Talk about hungry for God! They just wanted what Jesus had, and their hungry hearts brought the Kingdom of Heaven down to earth.

What was it about Jesus that made Him so irresistible? It was the presence of God, the Holy Spirit. The people could almost smell it! Imagine it like this—what is your favorite food? Cookies? Cake? Pizza? What happens when you get a whiff of that food cooking or baking? Does your mouth water and your stomach rumble? Do you get so hungry that you can't think about anything else but taking a nice, big bite of that delicious food? It's right there, driving you crazy—are you thinking about heading off to go do something else right now? Are you crazy? Most of us are probably just waiting for the word *go* so we can dig in!

Hunger for God opens our faith eyes to see the Kingdom, right? Well, that's not all it does! When you're hungry for God's presence in your life, it'll change your attitude. Bad attitudes like selfishness, complaining, and arguing are no fun to be around. Do you like hanging out with people like that? Wouldn't you rather have friends who are helpful, kind, and patient? If you want friends like that, *be* a friend like that! How? By keeping your eyes fixed on the Kingdom! Your attitude will just get better and better as you keep hungering for God's presence.

Hungry hearts also made us humble. God loves humble hearts, because people like that know how much they need God. People who realize they can't make it without God are in the best position to accept His gifts. Gifts like what? His Kingdom! Our big heavenly Dad loves to give His Kingdom to hungry people!

For the people following Jesus, getting an attitude change was like putting on 3D glasses when they used to only see in 2D. Now, they could start to see God's invisible world. Once this happened, Jesus could start to talk about the next attitude changes that would help the people get hold of even more of His Kingdom:

> *You will be blissfully happy if you are humble* [not full of yourself], *for you will receive the earth.*
>
> *You will be blissfully happy if you are hungry and thirsty for God and what is right, for you will get filled up.*
>
> *You will be blissfully happy if you show mercy* [to those who need forgiveness, instead of punishing them], *because you will get mercy when you need it.*
>
> *You will be blissfully happy if you are pure in heart* [a heart that loves God and hates sin], *for you will see God.*

You will be blissfully happy if you are a peacemaker, for you will be called a child of God.

You will be blissfully happy even when people make fun of you for loving God and doing what is right, for you get to have the Kingdom of Heaven (Matthew 5:5-11 paraphrased).

Check out the payout you get from these new attitudes—God's Kingdom, mercy, happiness, seeing God, and lots more! This is huge, because a lot of people think Jesus was just teaching people a bunch of boring rules. Do this—or else! But that's not what He was going for at all. He was sharing with us the ways to receive God's best gifts—His *blessings!*

We can have all those blessings, *plus* another gift—the amazing gift of *grace.* God's grace helps us to do more than just put on a good show—it lets us *be* the attitudes. The Father wants to see us become just like His Son, Jesus.

Two Kingdoms

The world that you *cannot* see with your eyes is more real and more powerful than the one you *can* see. If Christians can't see and receive His Kingdom, guess what? There is another kingdom, the kingdom of darkness, and it's going to cause some problems. The kingdom of darkness is invisible too, until you see the results it produces—the people who are sick, suffering, angry, hateful, prejudiced, poor, jobless, desperate, afraid, abused, outcast, lonely, and dying for love.

That's a pretty awful list, but the truth is you don't have to be afraid of this evil kingdom. Here's why: "His Kingdom rules over all" (Ps. 103:19 AMP). *All* means everything! You name it—God's Kingdom is bigger and stronger!

Jesus also said, "If I cast out demons by the Spirit of God, then the Kingdom of God has come upon you" (Matt. 12:28 NASB). Jesus only did miracles through God's power, the Holy Spirit, and the Kingdom of God comes in when someone is set free from the devil. It is like two armies in a battle—darkness versus light. Guess which one wins every single time? Duh! God's Kingdom of light, no contest. Darkness disappears in the light!

When I was a teenager, a group of us went on a tour of a huge cave. There were many lights all along the path as we descended into the caverns. We were all having a good time exploring. When we got to the deepest part of the cave, our guide had us stop, then he reached over and turned off the lights. It was unbelievably dark! I couldn't see anything, not even my hand in front of my face. You could almost *feel* the darkness. It was really strange, and kind of creepy. Nobody dared to move. Then the guide lit one little match. That tiny bit of light was like the sun had just entered the cave. It was a relief to be able to see again! The guide turned all the lights back on and the darkness vanished. Of course, once we could see again, no one was afraid to walk forward.

The point of that story is that you need faith in order to see how powerful the unseen world is, otherwise you can't do anything. In the next chapter, we're going to talk about how to use the gift of faith to bring God's Kingdom to earth.

Time with Your King

Your Father wants to show you His invisible world. It's the Kingdom of God.

If you want to see it, you will. God will help you to repent and change the way you think about things.

Close your eyes and ask your heavenly Father to come to you right now. He will show Himself to you.

Even if your eyes are closed, you will see things. You will see God. You will even see things that are in Heaven.

Your hunger for God will open your faith eyes.

God loves your hungry heart. You will discover great things about God and His Kingdom.

Ask the Father to help change your attitude. He will. Just receive it, and thank Him.

Journal Time

1. Write about what you saw when your eyes were closed.

2. What did God show you? Did you see God? Did you see things in Heaven?

3. Write about what the Kingdom of God looks like.

Mission Objectives

When you go to school or hang out with your friends, is God showing you things? If you see a sick person, what do you really *see?*

How can you show God's love and goodness to someone who might be angry or sad?

Ask God to show you someone, and do whatever God wants you to do to show His love. What happened?

Write about how God is changing your attitude.

Chapter 4

FAITH: THE EYES OF YOUR HEART

Some friends were visiting us one afternoon when we heard a knock on the door. It was a young mother who looked very worried. In her arms was her 6-month-old son. The baby was struggling to breathe and was crying. The mom was on her way to the hospital but wanted us to pray first. We gathered around them and began to pray. After a few minutes there was no change that we could see.

As she was about to leave, my son walked into the room, and we asked him to pray for the baby. As soon as he began to pray, everyone in the room felt something change. My son calmly continued to pray out loud with power and authority. When he was done, we opened our eyes, and what we saw was amazing. The baby was asleep, breathing without any problem!

The grateful mother took her baby home and put him to bed. My son had seen what was in Heaven, and his faith brought down healing and peace into our living room that day! He was only *five years old* at the time.

As a son or daughter of God, you have been given a powerful gift—the gift of *faith*. With this power, you will be able to see different worlds and different kingdoms that can't be seen with physical sight. Faith gives you spiritual eyes. With these eyes you can see what is invisible to everyone else. Many people think that this sort of thing is a special gift for only certain people. That is not true—anybody can have it, just like anybody can use their eyes to see!

If you are saved, you already have faith. Through faith you were saved, forgiven of sin, and became a Christian. With faith you believed in God, received His love, and asked His Son, Jesus, into your heart. (Read Ephesians 2:8.) You did not see Jesus physically, with your eyes, did you? But because of faith you can still know that God is real and you are His. You're in His family and His Kingdom. But that's just the beginning. Faith lets you see God's Kingdom and enjoy it every day!

What the Bible Says

Check out these Bible verses that really help you use those faith eyes:

> *Seek the Kingdom of God above all else, and live righteously, and He will give you everything you need* (Matthew 6:33).

Think about the things of heaven, not the things of earth (Colossians 3:2).

So we don't look at the troubles we can see now; rather, we fix our gaze on things that cannot be seen. For the things we see now will soon be gone [temporary], *but the things we cannot see will last forever* [everlasting] (2 Corinthians 4:18).

God's Word is inviting you to come and look into a world that is invisible. That's what Jesus did. He looked into Heaven, saw what His Father was doing, and then did the same thing on earth. (Read John 5:19.) That's when miracles happened—when Heaven came to earth. How did Jesus see into Heaven? With His *faith eyes!*

The Best Teacher Ever

God is on a mission—He wants you to activate that spiritual x-ray vision and see His Kingdom with your faith eyes. To make this happen, He sent you a teacher, the Holy Spirit, who is here to help. The Holy Spirit will act as a guide, taking you to brand new places where you can practice *seeing.* One of your first lessons will be *worship.* Worship helps you see God, and the Holy Spirit is here to teach you about true worship. In that place, where you are loving and praising God, you will begin to see the things that are invisible to the rest of the world, like God's throne—the center of His Kingdom. God will show you things that will blow your mind and stun your eyes, and it will be awesome. That's just what happens in God's presence.

Just about anyone who knows a little about the Bible has heard of David. We often remember him for killing lions, bears, and the giant, Goliath. He's known for being a shepherd and the king of Israel. But do you know what God remembers David for? David was a worshiper! His greatest passion was to be close to the Father. He learned how to see God's Kingdom, and he knew that God's presence was always with him. David saw God every single day with eyes of faith—every time he worshiped God.

As you worship God more often, your eyes of faith will get sharper. It will get easier and more natural for you to see the invisible things God wants to show you.

Seeing the Unseen

The invisible world is greater than the visible world. The closer you are to God and the better you know Him, the stronger your faith will become. So for example, if you believe that God might sometimes give people sickness, would you pray for a sick person to be healed? Even if you did pray for them, how strongly would you believe that God is going to heal them, if you aren't even sure that God wants to heal them? But if you know that God heals and only gives good things to people, you'll probably have a lot more faith for miracles. That's the kind of faith you get when you are close to Him— close enough to know for sure that He is a *good, good God!*

So, what's the opposite of faith? It's *unbelief*. Unbelief lives in the visible world. When people trust what they see, feel, and hear *more* than what their heart tells them, they are *unbelieving* in the invisible Kingdom of God and *believing* in a world that won't last long. (Read 1 Corinthians 7:31.) Of course, people who live by faith also know that what they see, feel, and hear is real. They just believe that the unseen world is *more* real.

Say that one day you go to school, the store, or the mall, and you see someone on crutches or in a wheelchair. What do you *see?* Unbelief sees someone who is hurt or crippled, maybe for the rest of their life. Unbelief says, "Oh, that is too bad." But what can you do? You just feel sorry for that person and walk away.

Faith sees something different, something more than your physical eyes can pick up on. Faith sees what God sees—a person who can be healed by God's power with a simple prayer. Faith sees what is happening in Heaven before it happens here on earth. Faith sees that person running and jumping. Jesus did amazing miracles because He saw His Father do it in Heaven first (look up John 5:19). Absolutely nobody is sick in Heaven! Everybody is healthy and strong, and that's the way it should be here on earth! The Kingdom of Heaven (the place you are *really* from) is greater and more powerful than what you see in this world.

Imagine a stabbing pain in your arm. Ow! You go to the doctor, and he says it's broken. It would be pretty silly to pretend your arm is fine. That's not faith; you're just lying to yourself. Real faith says, "Yeah, it's true, I have a broken arm. But what is *more* true is that Jesus took all my pain and sickness away 2,000 years ago. I can be healed!" (Check out 1 Peter 2:24.) There are no broken arms in Heaven, so your faith can drag healing down from Heaven to earth.

Don't Be Afraid

Have you ever had nightmares, or maybe just a weird feeling that something bad might happen tomorrow? That's called fear, and it's the devil's favorite thing to give you. In a negative way, fear is also faith in the unseen world—the kingdom of darkness. Fear is believing that bad things are going to happen before they ever do. It also starts when you believe the lies that the devil whispers, like, "Your best friend is going to stop talking to you and start being best friends with that person who hates you." When you get to thinking about these things and eventually believe they're true—that's when you are agreeing with the devil and his lies. That's when fear gets into your heart.

So how do you keep yourself free from fear? Stay in God's presence. The closer you are to your heavenly Dad, the more you will be surrounded by His peace, like a warm blanket. He will beat back the little lies that try to start fear in your heart and mind. He promised! (Read Philippians 4:7.)

Have you ever been laughed at because of what you said or did? Doesn't it feel terrible? Just knowing that people might laugh, mock, or reject us sometimes keeps us from doing something we feel is right. That's when unbelief can get started.

Are you ever afraid that people will make fun of you for having faith and believing God? They just don't know what you know about Him. But you know what? It's much better to fear God than people. Does fearing God mean you should be afraid of your heavenly Father? No way! It means to respect, trust, and obey Him. When you choose to believe that God is awesome and that nothing is impossible with Him, your faith gets a power boost. All that fear of what other people think about you will start running for its life!

Hanging Out with a Friend

The thing about faith is that you can't create it yourself. The Holy Spirit puts faith in your heart. (Read Ephesians 2:8.) You can't even imagine how powerful faith really is—mostly because it isn't something you grasp with your mind. Faith is when you know in your *heart* that you believe in God and you belong to Him. The power of faith comes from *agreeing with God*. The first sin involved Adam and Eve agreeing with the lies of the devil—negative faith. The results were a huge deal—death, separation from God, and evil getting into the world and ruining everything. On the other hand, when you agree by faith with God, the results are just as powerful, and overwhelmingly *good!*

Your Father wants you to tackle each day with faith, using that spiritual x-ray vision. The good news is that you won't have to do it alone. You have the best friend ever, the Holy Spirit, living in your heart. If you ask Him, He will tell you things and show you what to do and where to go. He will help you understand what you're dealing with. Spend more time with the Holy Spirit, and you'll learn how to tell when He's talking.

Promise and Proof

Not only does faith let you see into God's Kingdom—it also drags things from Heaven down to earth. This verse is huge: "Faith is the confidence that what we hope for will actually happen; it gives us assurance about things we cannot see" (Heb. 11:1). Let's say it another way: Faith (seeing with your spiritual vision) is the *promise* of getting what you are hoping for, and the *proof* that you will get it before you see it actually appear.

Here's how it works. Let's say you and your friends go out to eat and order a pizza. You pay for it and get your receipt with the number of your order on it. As you sit down at a table and wait, you place the number on the table where the server can see it. That number is the promise that you will get what you are hoping for—the pizza, exactly as you ordered.

If someone walks by and says, "Oh, your number isn't any good," you'd show them the receipt with that dollar amount on there—the money you paid for the pizza. The receipt is *proof* that you will get what you ordered, even though the pizza is still in the oven. When the pizza is ready, the server looks for the number on the table and brings the pizza to you.

So how do you receive things from Heaven? God looks for your number—your faith—and then He blesses you with incredible gifts from Heaven. Your Father honors and respects your faith. When you use your faith, you're saying, "Dad, I trust and believe in You. Your Kingdom has all that I need." What happens next? Faith moves Heaven to earth.

Heroes of Faith

God's Word is full of amazing heroes who did impossible things for God, even though they were just regular people who had faith and believed in Him. By faith:

- Noah built the ark (see Gen. 5–9).

- Abraham received God's promises and became the father of many nations (see Gen. 12).

- Moses parted the Red Sea (see Exod. 14).

- Daniel was protected in the lion's den (see Dan. 6).

- Joshua saw the walls of Jericho fall (see Josh. 6).

Stunning things happen when people act on their faith. God is still looking for more heroes. Any takers? Step up!

Like a Rope

So if the Holy Spirit gives us faith, the question is—*how?* In Romans 10:17 it says, "So faith comes from hearing, that is, hearing the Good News about Christ." That's your starting point. *Hear* what the Father says to you each day, and just like that your faith and trust in Him will grow. Spending time with your heavenly Dad is more important than it seems. It is critical that you *read* God's Word each day and *hear* what He is saying all day long. Your Father is always talking to you. Just pick up the "faith phone" and listen!

When you use your faith, you *delight* God. (Read Hebrews 11:6.) Using your faith shows Him that you trust God more than you trust what you see happening on earth. Anything you could possibly need is already in Heaven, just waiting to be given to you. Your faith is like a rope that can reach up to Heaven and lasso your answer.

Heaven hears your faith and answers. God will do amazing things. Miracles will happen—blind people will see and crippled people will walk. The enemy's kingdom will lose serious ground, and the Kingdom of Heaven will come to earth.

Change Inside Out

Keep watching Heaven with your faith eyes—something will happen to you. You'll have more courage. You won't be afraid to bring Heaven down to help people. You won't be shy when the Holy Spirit asks you to pray for someone. You'll believe that *nothing* is impossible with God!

Read Matthew 9:20-22. The woman in this story was sick for 12 years! How old were you 12 years ago? Can you imagine being sick that long? Read this story about how her faith gave her courage to touch Jesus. When she did, Heaven opened up, and she was healed of a sickness no amount of money and no doctor could cure.

You are a prince or princess, a royal son or daughter of the King. He showers you with treasures, because you are a rich treasure to Him. You've got the keys of authority and power to rule over the earth, and one royal mission—bring God's Kingdom of peace, healing, and joy to earth. Faith makes all this possible. How cool is that?

In the next chapter, you will discover how to use your faith to bring lightning down from Heaven—with prayer.

Time with Your King

Welcome your friend, the Holy Spirit. He lives within you always to give you power.

Ask Him to take you to your Father's throne in Heaven. He will do it.

See His throne. Ask the Holy Spirit to lead you into worship.

Thank the Father for all He has done for you. See Him with your heart.

Tell the Father how much you love Him.

Come closer to His throne. Climb up on His lap. Feel His love for you.

Let Him show you who He is and what He is like. You will see that He is good. He has good gifts. Look at them.

Your faith will grow. You can believe that God will do amazing things for people.

Journal Time

1. Write about what the Holy Spirit showed you and what you saw in Heaven.

2. What did it feel like to be so close to your heavenly Dad?

3. Describe the Father's goodness and His gifts.

Mission Objectives

As you set out on your daily mission, remember your friend, the Holy Spirit, is with you.

Listen to what He says. He will lead you and tell you when to use your faith.

Write down what you saw with the eyes of your faith. Was it different from what your eyes see?

Did your faith reach up to Heaven and bring down something that was needed on earth? Write what it was and what happened.

Chapter 5

LIGHTNING FROM HEAVEN

It was just another Wednesday night at church. About 20 kids showed up for our weekly Global Fire class. I had an idea what God wanted to do that night, but He did not tell me everything. He likes to surprise us.

I made a large circle of flags from different nations on the floor, and then gathered the boys and girls to sit inside. The mission tonight was to find out what was on God's heart for the nations, and then pray for whatever He showed us. What happened next was incredible.

We started to worship and love on our heavenly Dad. It felt like Heaven opened up, and God's presence flooded the room. The kids started praying out loud with all their heart and might. Soon, every one of them was lying face down on the floor, and some began to cry out for God to touch the people, to save and heal them. Then I took all the flags and covered the kids with them.

As their prayers were getting stronger, my spiritual x-ray vision activated, and I saw more than a thousand people being saved and set free from the devil! This went on for another half hour. By now, it was getting late, and parents were coming to pick up their kids. As they walked in the room, the moms and dads fell backward and just sat down on the floor. God's presence in the room was overwhelming!

When I felt the Lord was done doing what He had planned, I asked the kids what God had shown them. Every one of them saw the same thing—large brick walls around cities and countries were breaking apart and falling down. People were running out from the walls laughing and singing. At the same time, I was seeing all those people getting touched by God and saved!

That night, the kids came into God's presence. They saw His heart, and He showed them how to agree with Him and pray. They obeyed and prayed. Heaven came down like lightning, and more than a thousand people came into the Kingdom of God.

Prayer is powerful!

Jesus Shows Us How to Pray

In Matthew 6, Jesus' disciples asked Him how they should pray. He taught them the famous prayer called the Lord's Prayer. In this prayer, Jesus wanted to teach two major things about prayer. First, when you worship God, you will become close to Him. Second, prayer brings Heaven to earth. When that happens, God's Kingdom comes and helps people.

As we get ready to look at this prayer, keep in mind—as one of God's kids, you are really from another world. Your royal mission is on this planet, but earth is not your home. The reason you are here is to show God's love and power to others.

Let's take a close look at the Lord's Prayer and see what we can find. (See Matthew 6:9-13 NKJV.)

Our Father in Heaven, hallowed be Your name.

When you call God, "Father," it honors Him. It shows the special, loving relationship He has with you. Just think about what God had to do to become your Dad. He gave you all He had—His Son and His love. Doesn't He deserve all your worship? The word *hallowed* means "to respect and praise." That's Heaven—a place of worship and praise. It's the most awesome concert in the universe! Don't you think we could use a little of that concert on earth, too? Worship is the number-one way to honor and respect God. Why? Because God *lives* in your praise. (Read Psalms 22:3.) God shows off His power when you tell Him how awesome He is. It makes Him so happy, and He deserves it more than anyone.

A 10-year-old boy named Dakota had very poor eyesight. At his young age, he already needed thick glasses to see. One Sunday during the worship service, his glasses began to fog up. He took them off to clean them, and he saw a bright light. He put his glasses back on, but everything was still foggy. He took them off again and looked around. He could see perfectly! No one prayed for him. He was just worshiping, and God healed him!

Miracles like that are fantastic, but we shouldn't be shocked by them. God hears us every time, and our praise and worship get Him excited to come help us out. Isaiah 42:12-13 says, "Let the whole world glorify the Lord; let it sing His praise. The Lord will march forth like a mighty hero; He will come out like a warrior, full of fury. He will shout His battle cry and crush all His enemies." So when you praise and worship God, all of Heaven hears and answers you. The Lord gets up from His royal throne, puts on His battle armor, and grabs His sword. Then He swoops down, lock on to your enemy, and fights the battle for you!

Your Kingdom come. Your will be done on earth as it is in heaven.

This is the most important thing for prayer. If the answer to the problem is in Heaven, then we need to bring it down here to earth.

You meet a sick person. Because you are close to God, He shows you His heart—He wants that person to be healed. Your faith *sees* that sickness being healed. When you pray for healing, you're letting loose a lightning bolt from Heaven— the powerful answer to the problem. When that lightning bolt hits the problem of sickness, it's a no-brainer. Sickness *dies*, and the person is healed.

What God wants is always happening in Heaven, and He wants to see all that good stuff happen here on earth too. That's your job. You get to help bring Heaven to earth. If something is not allowed in Heaven, then we can't allow it here on earth either. Better handcuff it and kick it out! Jesus said, "I tell you the truth, whatever you forbid on earth will be forbidden in heaven, and whatever you permit on earth will be permitted in heaven" (Matt. 18:18). When you pray like that, you are using your keys of authority and power. All of the power in Heaven is waiting to help you.

How much Heaven stuff are we trying to bring to earth? No one really knows, but the Bible says it is more than you can even dream or think about. Look up Ephesians 3:20.

Give us this day our daily bread.

Is there anyone starving in Heaven? Of course not! God's Kingdom on earth means people will have all they need. God is a good Dad who loves to give His kids all the best. And if we are on a mission to help others who are hungry and poor, He's even more excited to give us everything we need for that. Philippians 4:19 says, "And this same God who takes care of me will supply all your needs from his glorious riches, which have been given to us in Christ Jesus." That's God's promise—to give us all we need. He's richer than a gazillionaire, and Heaven is like His crazy-huge mansion. We can live in the mansion right here and now!

And forgive us our debts, as we forgive our debtors.

Is there any anger, fighting, or unforgiveness in Heaven? Not likely! It is a place overflowing with peace and love—the perfect example of how we should treat each other here on earth. The Bible says, "Instead, be kind to each other, tender-hearted, forgiving one another, just as God through Christ has forgiven you" (Eph. 4:32).

A *debt*, like an IOU, is when you owe someone. It could be a little favor or a big chunk of cash. We all have a debt called *sin*, and none of us could pay the price—that's why Jesus paid it for us. Thanks to Him, we're forgiven by God, so now we can forgive other people when they hurt us. Forgiving someone who doesn't deserve it shows them what God's love is like. It's a taste of the Kingdom!

And do not lead us into temptation, but deliver us from the evil one.

There is no temptation or sin in Heaven—it's gone, along with all the evil. When you get connected up to God's Kingdom and keep Him close, sin and evil run for their lives!

James 1:13 says it is impossible for God to tempt you. That is what the devil does. The Lord's Prayer doesn't work without *grace*. Your Father gives you grace so you have the power to stay close to Him. With grace in hand, you'll always know how much you need God's presence!

When your heart is close to God, the devil loses big time. The Bible says, "So humble yourselves before God. Resist the devil, and he will flee from you" (James 4:7). In other words, give yourself to God, turn away from the devil, and he'll just take off running!

Did you know that it's possible to be so close to your heavenly Dad that you don't even give the devil the time of day? At the first sign of temptation, you'll just say, "Forget it," and the devil will do a one-eighty and run!

For Yours is the Kingdom and the power and the glory forever. Amen.

When you say these words from the Lord's Prayer, you are praising God. Your Father owns Heaven—that's why He can give you His Kingdom. The Bible is loaded with praise for God, because "all glory and power is His." Your heavenly Dad loves to hear it! And why not? If you love someone, doesn't it give you warm tingles to hear them say they like you too? So here's an idea—when you pray, spend a good chunk of time just praising God. It's the best part of your prayer!

Finding the Kingdom

> *But seek first the kingdom of God and His righteousness, and all these things shall be added to you* (Matthew 6:33 NKJV).

In this Scripture verse, Jesus is giving us a hint for praying powerful prayers. He says seek (or find) His Kingdom *first!* Always ask God what He's doing *first.* Ask the Father what would please Him. Here's another hint—He likes to give us the good things from His Kingdom.

When you pray, why are you doing it? God would like to hear prayers for people to see Jesus and His Kingdom. When the Kingdom of God gets inside a sin-filled person, the sin is gone—forgiveness takes its place. When God's power smacks into sickness and disease, people are healed. Yeah God! When He finds demon-tormented people—you know it! They are set free from their fears and dark thoughts. God's Kingdom heals every part of a person—spirit, soul/mind, and body. Praise God!

Get that prayer focus on God's Kingdom *first*, and it'll be pretty obvious that Heaven is overflowing with everything people need.

Secrets in the Heart

Prayer is like a really tight hug with your heavenly Dad. It's squished-together, nothing-between-us closeness. It's where you need to be, because when God wants to tell you the secrets that are in His heart, He doesn't shout them across the room; He whispers in your ear. When you hear His heart about something, just pray it back to Him. He loves to hear you echoing His heart, because that's when you and God are on the same page.

The power of prayer is amazing. It's like God is just waiting for His people to pray so He can jump into action. He *likes* to answer your prayers! He has decided to do His will and bring His Kingdom to earth through *you* and through your prayers.

What would happen if God's people didn't pray? The kingdom of darkness would rule over the earth. That is why the devil is scared to death of anyone who knows how to pray—even teens and little kids!

From Another World

What country were you born in? If you're living there, then you are a citizen of that country. As a citizen, you probably speak the language, wear the clothes, and eat the food from that country.

Paul said something pretty wild, "We are citizens of heaven, where the Lord Jesus Christ lives. And we are eagerly waiting for Him to return as our Savior" (Phil. 3:20). Paul was not talking about going to Heaven someday, but living as a citizen of Heaven *today*. That means you think, see, talk, and act like you're in Heaven right now!

If you've ever visited another country, you might have noticed that the people dress, talk, and live a little differently. In the same way, you're paying a visit to earth, but you're really a citizen of another world—God's Kingdom of Heaven!

Not only are you a citizen of Heaven, you are an ambassador of Heaven too. (Read 2 Corinthians 5:20.) An ambassador officially represents his country while living in another country. As Heaven's ambassador, you represent Heaven here on earth. An ambassador also gets his paycheck from the country he represents, not the country he is living in. As an ambassador of Heaven, you get paid with the riches of Heaven. God's writing the checks, and He will take care of you and make sure you have whatever you need. No worries!

If an ambassador is ever in danger, the army from his home country will protect him. There are soldiers assigned to help him do his job. For His ambassador from Heaven, God provides an army of angels, armed and ready to help you complete your royal mission!

This is what it means to be from another world. You are what Heaven looks, talks, thinks, and acts like. You're equipped with Heaven's riches, God's love, and His presence. The keys of power and authority are in your hands, and you're all set to pray His Kingdom down to earth.

Time with Your King

Being in God's presence to worship Him is the first part of prayer.

Begin to praise your Father for what He has done for you. Thank Him for all His good gifts. Now just worship Him.

Tell Him how great He is. Tell Him how much you love Him. Ask Him what is in His heart.

Be still; come closer to Him. Listen for His whisper. Listen for His heartbeat. He will show you what to pray.

Begin to pray what you saw and heard from your heavenly Dad.

Enjoy being this close to Him. He will tell you how pleased He is with you. Thank Him and love on Him.

Journal Time

1. What did you hear when you listened to your Father's heart?

2. What did your eyes of faith see when He showed you what to pray?

3. What did it feel like being so close to your heavenly Dad?

4. Write about the things you heard and saw with your heart.

Mission Objectives

How can you be an ambassador from Heaven?
Look for ways you can represent Heaven:

- At home,

- When you're hanging out,

- At school,

- To someone who is sick, injured, or hurting.

Write about what happened when you acted like an ambassador.

Chapter 6

THE KINGDOM AND THE SPIRIT

It was our first family mission trip. My wife, two sons (who were young boys at the time), and I were invited to Mexico. We were going to minister at a school that had several hundred kids. We started by teaching about God, the Holy Spirit, and what He wants to do in our lives. Kids were being touched and blessed by God's presence, but it was only the beginning. The Holy Spirit had a surprise for us.

After the first meeting, we started going around to the classrooms. As we walked into the first room, I felt the Holy Spirit come in with us. I told everyone the Holy Spirit was with us and that He wanted to fill their hearts. I explained that when the Holy Spirit fills their hearts, they will speak in different languages as the Spirit praises God. The kids closed their eyes, and I prayed. As we touched each of them, one by one they were filled with the Holy Spirit. God's presence was wonderful!

One boy, Roberto, was standing by himself off in the corner, watching. We were told that he was struggling in school and wasn't very happy. I walked over to Roberto and heard the Holy Spirit say, "When you touch Roberto, I will fill him with My presence."

I told Roberto, "You're going to receive the Holy Spirit." I smiled and touched him, and just like that, Roberto fell into a chair and started speaking in another language.

Minutes later, all the children were on the floor, praising God in other languages—"tongues," as the Bible calls them. As we headed for the next class, I looked back and saw Roberto under his desk, praising God with all his might, a huge smile glowing on his face. We went to the next classroom, the Holy Spirit right there with us.

The Holy Spirit showed up that day in a powerful way. God filled the kids with Himself—the best gift in the world.

The Greatest Prophet

If you had to guess, who do you think was the greatest person in the Bible? Abraham was a pretty big deal; so was Moses. How about King David? There were some incredible prophets who did awesome miracles, like Isaiah, Daniel, and Elijah. Guess who Jesus thought was the greatest. John the Baptist. John didn't do any miracles, but Jesus called him the greatest of all the prophets.

So who was this guy John?

John was Jesus' cousin, and he was a bit crazy. Most people thought so anyway, because he lived in the desert, wore animal skins, and ate bugs. You can see why they thought he was nuts. But he was a prophet, and he baptized people and told them to repent—the Lamb of God was coming to take sin out of the world (look up Matt, 3:2 and John 1:29). The Holy Spirit told John that his cousin, Jesus, was the Savior. John told the people, "Someone is coming soon who is greater than I am…He will baptize you with the Holy Spirit and with fire [power]" (Matt. 3:11).

One day, Jesus showed up at the River Jordan, where John was baptizing people. Jesus walked into the water and asked John to baptize Him. John said, "I am the one who needs to be baptized by You…so why are You coming to me?" (Matt. 3:13-14). But Jesus insisted, so John went ahead and baptized Him.

As Jesus was getting out of the river, Heaven opened up, and God (the Holy Spirit) came down to Jesus in the form of a dove. At that moment, the heavenly Father spoke in a loud voice and said, "This is My dearly loved Son, who brings Me great joy" (Matt. 3:17). From then on, the Holy Spirit was with Jesus, giving Him all the power He needed to change the world!

John was here for all this, proclaiming to everyone that Jesus was the Savior of the world. He had heard from God, and he knew how important the Holy Spirit was. That's what made John the greatest prophet. But here's the thing—Jesus said that the *least* famous person in the Kingdom of God is greater than John the Baptist! (Read Matthew 11:11.) Why? Well, because Jesus gives His followers something that no prophet or king in the Bible ever had, not even John. It's the baptism of the Holy Spirit, and God gives it to any person who asks for it, whether they seem important or not. God just wants *everyone* to have His Spirit!

A New Language

Jesus came to earth for two vital reasons. The first was to pay the price for our sin so we could be forgiven. The second was so every Christian could be filled with the Holy Spirit. God wants every person to be overflowing with *Himself!* As the Bible puts it, "Then you will be made complete with all the fullness of life and power that comes from God" (Eph. 3:19).

In the Bible, when people started to get filled and baptized with the Holy Spirit, it was incredible. Miracles happened, God's power was obvious, and people started speaking in different languages (or tongues). Speaking in tongues is when you have a special language that your spirit uses to speak to God. Your mind doesn't understand it, but that's okay. Praising God in tongues blesses Him and tells Him how great He is (look up Acts 2:11). It makes His day! You get a lot out of it too. The Bible says that praying in the Holy Spirit, in tongues, makes your spirit strong (read Jude 20). You get supplied with power, like a spiritual energy drink!

Some people think that when they get filled with the Holy Spirit they just speak in tongues and that's it. Nope! There's more—lots more!

Holy Spirit: Power and Presence

Jesus did not perform a single miracle—no healings and no demons cast out—until He was baptized in the Holy Spirit. He needed God's power to do what the Father asked of Him. You better believe you need the same power to complete *your* royal mission.

The power of the Holy Spirit in you chases away the kingdom of darkness with God's Kingdom of light. When that happens, people are set free from the darkness of sin, sickness, depression, and hatred. The kingdom of darkness always has to beat it when God's light of healing, joy, and love shows up. Just as a light bulb needs electricity to shine, the Holy Spirit powers God's light.

God is so good, and He has so many wonderful gifts for you. But the greatest gift is the Holy Spirit Himself. The Holy Spirit *in* you lets you get up close and personal with God. People in the Old Testament did some wild things because of God's promise, "the Lord your God is with you wherever you go" (Josh. 1:9):

- Moses brought the Israelites out of Egypt.

- Joshua led the Israelites into the Promised Land.

- Gideon led a war.

Jesus told His disciples to "go and make disciples of all the nations" (Matt. 28:19). Then He promised them that He would stick with them forever, no matter what. God's presence is what makes impossible things happen. He's going to make your royal mission a success—He promised.

The Holy Spirit's *presence* shows people what God's Kingdom is really like. Peter walked around with the presence of the Holy Spirit, and people were healed just because he got close. It wasn't Peter's shadow magically healing people—it was the shadow of the Holy Spirit. (Read Acts 5:15.) Jesus had the presence of the Holy Spirit, too. People who just touched His clothes were healed. (Read Mark 6:56.)

Follow the Leader

When I was a kid, I used to play "Follow the Leader" with my friends. One person was the leader, and the rest of us had to follow anywhere and everywhere. It was fun for us as kids because we had no idea where we were going—only the leader knew. It was kind of an adventure as we followed the leader over rocks, under bushes, and around trees. The fun was just keeping up.

It's just like life, when you're following the Leader, the Holy Spirit. He knows where to go and what to do. He's got the ideas, whether it's praying for someone or doing something that seems kind of strange. Just trust Him and do what He asks. This makes our faith fun and exciting—the Leader can be pretty spontaneous! But that's life when you're baptized in the Holy Spirit. That's how Jesus did it, and His life was wild!

Filled and Refilled

Can you be baptized in the Holy Spirit only once? Nope! The Bible says that the followers of Jesus were filled with the Holy Spirit, but they were also filled again (check out Acts 2 and Acts 8).

Why? Are we leaking Holy Spirit or something? Actually—yes! Just like a plant needs water to grow, you are going to need a fresh "drink" of the Holy Spirit from time to time. If you played sports or worked outside on a hot summer day, wouldn't you get hot and thirsty? You'd definitely be looking for a refreshing, cold drink. If you pray for people and give away God's love to others, you'll need to get filled up again. You can't give something away if you are empty. Besides, it's fun to soak up more and more of God's presence and love. And He has fun pouring out His Spirit on you!

So get your free refill of the Holy Spirit every day!

Time with Your King

Jesus wants you to have everything He has—everything! He even wants you to have His very Spirit, His own presence.

Close your eyes and invite God's presence. Ask Him to fill you with His Holy Spirit. He is a free gift; He will come to you.

Let Him fill you up, so much that you feel like He is overflowing in you.

Feel His presence in you...welcome Him. Feel His joy... thank Him. Let your spirit, not your mind, thank Him.

Let your heart tell Him how great and wonderful He is. It's okay if you don't understand the words you are speaking. It's called speaking in tongues.

Your heart knows. God knows. He understands your words, and He is pleased!

Enjoy what is happening. This is only the beginning. Speaking in tongues can be a big part of your friendship with God. Your heart wants to talk to God in tongues all the time.

Practice, practice, practice every day.

Journal Time

1. After you have enjoyed this time with the Holy Spirit, write about what it was like to be filled to overflowing.

2. How did it feel to be so close to God?

3. How did your heavenly Father feel about this time with you?

Mission Objectives

Now that you have experienced the Holy Spirit this way, do you feel like you have more courage?

Do you feel like you are not alone, but have God's presence and strength in you?

Do you feel you can do things that you were afraid to do before?

Share what happened with your parents and friends.

Write down how things seem different now. Write the things that the Holy Spirit is saying to you.

Chapter 7

SMEARED WITH GOD

The youth group went to an amusement park just to have fun for the day. For the first two hours they were having a blast, hanging out, and riding the rides. Then, two boys noticed a man with a cast on his arm, and they started chatting with him. The man said he injured his arm at work, and he was in a lot of pain. The boys prayed for him, and after a few seconds they told him to see if the arm felt any better. The man started to move and bend it. "Oh my gosh!" he shouted, "It's all better!" His wife was ecstatic. Now the boys were starting to notice people who needed prayer all over the place.

After a few more miracles, the excited boys met up with their group and told them what God had done. They asked the other kids if they wanted to see some miracles today. Everyone said yes, and the two boys put their hands on the teenagers and prayed for them. Then they all split up to pray for people in the park.

The rest of the youth group said that when the two boys prayed for them, they felt courage and were not nervous at all. By the end of the day, the youth saw several people who were in wheelchairs get up and walk without pain! God used the youth group in a great way, because those two boys gave to their friends what they had—God's power and the anointing of the Holy Spirit.

Power for the Plan

The heavenly Father gave His Son a royal mission. Jesus came to make a way for everyone to find the Father. He also planned to show the world who the Father really was by showing them what Heaven was like.

This would only work if Jesus could do powerful things like miracles. For powerful miracles, He needed power to make them happen. That power was God, the Holy Spirit. Jesus needed the Holy Spirit *in* Him and *on* Him. When the Holy Spirit touches a person, we say that person is "anointed." The word *anoint* actually means "to smear or cover." In Bible days, when someone started out as a king or prophet, they would be anointed with oil. Oil was poured out and smeared all over the person to show that they were ready for the job.

Jesus, the Anointed One

The very name *Jesus Christ* means "Jesus, the anointed one." It was this anointing that helped Jesus do what He saw His Father doing in Heaven. It was this anointing that caused all of those powerful miracles. People saw and smelled the Holy Spirit power on Jesus. That's what they wanted. That's why they left everything behind to follow Him.

This anointing terrifies the devil and wrecks his kingdom of darkness. He will do anything he can to kill the anointing. He tried when Jesus was on earth, and that's why the religious leaders had Jesus put to death.

The devil doesn't care if people think Jesus was just a teacher or a good man who tried to help people. But he cares big time about God's power—it freaks him out! Even today he whispers the lie, "Oh, those miracles that Jesus did were only for Bible times, not for today." Or he'll say, "It is the devil who did those miracles you hear about today." Seems silly of him to try to take credit for putting holes in his kingdom of darkness, doesn't it?

So why is the devil afraid of God's power? Because the anointing breaks the chains of sickness, fear, and hatred that the devil tortures people with. The anointing wins! The anointing, or the actions of the Holy Spirit, is what invites people into God's Kingdom.

If Jesus needed the anointing of the Holy Spirit, what about you?

Jesus Sends the Holy Spirit

Jesus told His disciples it was actually better for them that He was leaving and going back to Heaven (look up John 16:7). The disciples were confused. How could Jesus going away be a good thing? But because He went back to Heaven, Jesus was able to send the Holy Spirit to all of His followers, all over the world.

The Book of Acts is full of exciting stories about how Jesus' disciples were full of the Holy Spirit and all the things they did. People were healed, raised from the dead, and set free from demons. When they brought God with them, it worked every time!

The Holy Spirit lives in your spirit. When He's in your spirit, you get to enjoy His presence and closeness. You can't even describe how awesome it is to be filled with His power.

Leaking the Holy Spirit

The anointing of the Holy Spirit takes the impossible and makes it possible. Last time I checked, we humans can't really do awesome, powerful healings and miracles by ourselves. We can't bring people back to life, make short limbs grow out to full length, or cure terminal illness. But with the anointing of God's Spirit, you can do the impossible and bring Heaven to earth.

Hopefully you're not thinking that the Holy Spirit sounds like a pushy boss who makes you do whatever He wants. He's the opposite! The Holy Spirit is a person who wants to be with you. Would you rather go hang out at the mall with your friends or by yourself? With friends, right? Being with people you like is fun! The Holy Spirit feels the same way—He wants to be friends with you, spend time together, and team up with you as a partner. He won't force you to do miracles—He'll just invite you, to see if you want to do something together with Him. Just say *yes!*

So, how does the Holy Spirit leak out of you to do powerful things? The Holy Spirit leaks out when:

You know His presence is in you. Getting filled up with Him over and over again is fantastic. (We'll go over this more in your "Time with Your King" at the end of this chapter.)

You have God's compassion for people. Compassion is more than just pitying someone who is sick or has a need. It is a powerful force that loves people and hates what the devil has done to them. Compassion is what moved Jesus and released the anointing to heal the sick and set people free from the devil.

You are willing to do what the Holy Spirit asks you to do. Maybe He will want you to pray for an older person who is sick or a friend at school who is having problems. Just do whatever He asks, and don't be afraid of what people will think. They'll change their minds when they see a miracle anyway!

You let the Father use you for those impossible things like miracles. See His power change things, and watch His Kingdom come.

This is what makes your royal mission so exciting and *possible!*

God's Word, God's Voice

God is always speaking to you; you just need to know how to hear Him. He usually speaks in one of two ways, and both are important. Sometimes He uses a "text message" (the Bible), and other times he talks to you directly with the quiet voice of His Holy Spirit.

You get to know God's voice when you hang out with Him, trust Him, and depend on Him. When you have a friend who calls you a lot, you get to know the sound of their voice. God's voice will become familiar, too. God's voice will always agree with His Word, the Bible. He wants you to know what's in His Book, so He'll help you understand what you read.

God is pouring out His Spirit like rain from Heaven. The more you get soaked and filled up, the better you will know His voice.

Time with Your King

As you invite the Holy Spirit to come, let Him soak and fill you with Himself. It will refresh you and make you feel alive inside.

It's like you are a plant that just had a drink of fresh water.

Feel His joy; it will give you strength. Hear what He says to you. You'll know that anything the Spirit asks you to do is possible.

Thank Him for His love, presence, and power that you have been given.

Journal Time

1. Write down the things you are learning about the Holy Spirit.

2. What does He look, sound, and feel like?

3. What does it feel like when He comes to fill you up?

4. Can you trust Him to lead you each day?

5. Did He show you something to do, like someone to pray for?

6. Write what the Holy Spirit wants you to do today.

7. Write what happened when you did it.

8. It is so much fun to write what God is doing through you! Write what you are feeling.

Mission Objectives

The Holy Spirit is *in* you for you to enjoy. The Holy Spirit is *on* you to help others.

Look for those who need to see and feel God's presence and power.

Be willing to let God use you.

Ask your friend and partner, the Holy Spirit, what He wants you to do.

Let His compassion move you.

Let the anointing give you power to do the impossible. Write about what happened when the Holy Spirit leaked out of you.

PART II

HEAVEN ON EARTH

Chapter 8

SHOW AND TELL

It was getting late. The big room upstairs at church was filled with more than 100 kids. God had done amazing things all week. The kids learned how to heal the sick, pray, and prophesy over people. We were now going to show a video and have everyone rest. As we were trying to get the TV to work, my wife whispered to me that a girl in our group was healed earlier that day. I thought, *Hmm, let's share some testimonies until the video is ready.*

Just then, I heard the Holy Spirit say, "Teach about words of knowledge."

I obeyed and taught for five minutes, giving the kids the basics on this gift of the Holy Spirit. Then the Holy Spirit said, "Now, let's show them how to do it."

I had the kids close their eyes and just ask the Holy Spirit for words of knowledge. We prayed, and then I asked, "Who heard something?" About 12 hands shot up. One by one the kids came up and told us where they felt a pain in their body. (That's one way God gives a word of knowledge for healing.) We then asked if anyone in the room had that kind of pain. When a hand went up, we would pray for healing. The results were 100 percent positive. *Everyone* we prayed for was healed!

About 45 minutes later, I said, "Wow! There must have been 30 healings tonight! Isn't God awesome?" One boy raised his hand and said, "There were actually 35 kids who were healed. I wrote each one down in my journal." The kids got a hands-on lesson in words of knowledge that night because they heard God's voice, saw His power, and felt His healing touch.

Show and Tell

Do you remember having Show and Tell in school? Those were pretty fun days, right? You didn't just *listen* to someone talking for a change—you got to *see* what they were talking about, touch it, and sometimes even taste! Jesus did something similar when He taught about the Kingdom of God. Whenever Jesus told people about His Father and what Heaven is like, He also showed them the evidence in powerful miracles. The Bible says:

> *Jesus traveled throughout the region of Galilee, teaching in the synagogues and announcing the Good News about the Kingdom. And He healed every kind of disease and illness* (Matthew 4:23).

Jesus traveled through all the towns and villages of that area, teaching in the synagogues and announcing the Good News about the Kingdom. And He healed every kind of disease and illness (Matthew 9:35).

Go and announce to them that the Kingdom of Heaven is near. Heal the sick, raise the dead, cure those with leprosy, and cast out demons. Give as freely as you have received! (Matthew 10:7-8).

Jesus was *not* a boring guy behind a podium! He was the coolest teacher you could ever have! He didn't want to just *tell* people about the Kingdom of God, He wanted to *show* them what the Kingdom felt, tasted, and smelled like. When the people heard Jesus teach and then saw Him do miracles, they got the message.

The Kingdom of God includes *seeing* and *feeling* God's presence. It also involves a lot of God's power. That is why Jesus had to show the presence and power of the Holy Spirit in miracles. Whenever you tell someone about the Kingdom, Heaven is ready to show up and show off. You and the Holy Spirit are a team, and you each do your part to win.

Big Heads or Big Hearts?

Things get a little messed up if people just *hear* about God's Kingdom and never see His presence and power. They get only a half-picture of the Kingdom of God. The apostle

Paul said that knowledge makes us "puffed up" (look up 1 Cor. 8:1 NKJV). If all we have is head knowledge, pride has a chance to take over our hearts and minds.

The Bible is the best book ever written. What could be better than a book about God, His love, and His Kingdom? It's got true stories, poetry, prophecy, and the best life advice you'll ever hear. Our heavenly Dad *really* wants us to dig in to His book and know what it says—but just *knowing* the Bible isn't enough. Even the devil knows what the Bible says!

Paul wrote, "For the Kingdom of God is not just a lot of talk; it is living by God's power" (1 Cor. 4:20). God's presence and power show the truth of the Word of God. That's what makes God's Word alive, and the living Word feeds your heart. Big hearts are much better than big heads!

Knowing God

Do you have a hero? Maybe someone famous you really like? How would you get to know a person like that? You could read a book or an article about them, watch them on TV or YouTube, or hear someone talk about them. You might do even better if you follow their Twitter. But the best thing of all would be if you could meet that person, or even live with them like a roommate! Wouldn't it be fun to go places and do things together? If you were their best friend, you would *really* know them the best. Well, there you go—that's how God is. Being a Christian is all about being as close as you can to a person—God.

Just like reading a famous person's blog, reading the Bible is how you find out what God is like. But that's just the beginning. God's Spirit and power take things to a whole new level, because you get to meet Him and learn firsthand about His Kingdom. Even better, you get to live with Him and be in His Kingdom. You're a part of God's family, living in His house!

So you're a Christian, and you're super close to God. Now what? Remember how Jesus taught the people and then did miracles and healings all over the place? The Holy Spirit was on Him, and everyone saw His power. That got them so hungry for Heaven that they followed Jesus—because they could see, feel, and smell the Kingdom on Him.

People don't want to just hear a nice message *about* God. When they see God doing things they can't explain with His power, people's lives change. That's where you come in.

A Map or a Guide?

Discovering God's Kingdom is like going on a treasure hunt. My friends and I used to make up maps and clues for each other and go on treasure hunts. Sometimes, though, it was hard to read the map and clues—bad drawings, bad handwriting, or clues that just didn't makes sense made it impossible for me to find the treasure. One time I even got lost trying to follow a map. It would have been a lot easier if the person who made the map were there to help me understand their crazy clues. Just a few hints, and I would have found the treasure for sure.

God's Word is like a treasure map with all the clues you need about God and His Kingdom—except His map is perfect, and we just have a hard time reading it sometimes. But God also gives you a guide—the Holy Spirit. Only He can explain the clues in the Bible. Go ahead and ask Him for help—your heavenly Dad doesn't mind at all. He'll see how hard you're looking and be thrilled to lend a hand. Remember, "It is God's privilege to conceal things and the king's privilege to discover them" (Prov. 25:2). The Holy Spirit will help you make those discoveries. When you read God's Word, He will feed your hungry heart—and the more the Holy Spirit feeds you from God's Word, the hungrier you will get!

God's Love Letter

It's all because God loves you so much that He gives you both a Guide and a map. Your Guide, the Holy Spirit, will lead you, show you, and give you power to be and do what His Word says.

Invite Holy Spirit along on your treasure hunt—then God's Word will lead you closer to Jesus. You'll feel like you need Him more and more, and you'll want to know Him and His power. When you read the Bible, it will be like reading a love letter from someone you adore.

Plus, you'll have the Spirit's power to do what Jesus did— tell others about the Kingdom of God, and then show it wherever you go.

Time with Your King

Take your Bible and find a quiet place. Ask the Holy Spirit to take you into Dad's presence. Thank your Dad for His love and goodness.

Tell Him how great He is and worship Him. Let Him love on you, and enjoy being so close to Him.

Now ask the Holy Spirit to show you things from God's Word. Open your Bible to Matthew, Mark, Luke, or John. Read about what Jesus said and did.

Let the Holy Spirit feed and bring your heart closer to Jesus. Read some more.

Take your time and see what Jesus wants to do. Thank Him for this time.

Journal Time

1. Write what the Holy Spirit showed you in God's Word.

2. What did you hear?

3. What did you see?

4. What did you feel when you were getting closer to Jesus?

5. Did reading God's Word seem different from usual? How?

Mission Objectives

Ask the Holy Spirit to show you someone who needs to know about the Kingdom of God.

The person may be at home, school, the mall, or the store. He will show you someone.

Tell that person about God's love and power. The Holy Spirit will be there with you.

Ask the person if you can pray for them.

Invite the Holy Spirit to fill them with God's love.

If the person has any pain, ask if you can pray for them.

After you pray, ask how they are feeling.

As they feel better, let them know it is God's power and love that they are feeling.

Write what happened.

Chapter 9

THE WORKS OF
THE FATHER

For hundreds of years, prophets were hearing from God and telling people that a King was coming to save them. They gave over 300 specific details about the Savior. They told people when He would come and what He would do.

The night Jesus was born, all Heaven exploded with joy and celebration. Angels appeared and announced, "The Savior—yes, the Messiah, the Lord—has been born today in Bethlehem, the city of David!" (Luke 2:11). Even outer space got in on the party, as a new star appeared in the night sky to guide the wise men to Jesus. That's no ordinary baby announcement!

Even though Jesus was the most important person ever to walk on earth—with a royal mission that would change the whole world—He said an amazing thing, "Don't believe Me unless I carry out My Father's work" (John 10:37). What was His proof? *Miracles!*

The Father's Business

Just like a lot of us, Jesus grew up with human parents. He had chores, went to school, and got a job—working with His dad as a carpenter. In the midst of this normal life, Jesus was finding out who He was and why He came to earth. He was here on a mission—to do the Father's business.

When Jesus was 12, He was separated from His mom and dad during a long trip out of town. His parents, Mary and Joseph, were frantic when they could not find Jesus—He was missing for several days. Finally, they found Him in the temple, *teaching* the priests and religious leaders! Jesus wasn't sorry when His parents showed up, a bit confused. All He said was, "Didn't you know that I must be in My Father's house?" (Luke 2:49).

Even though Jesus was a good kid and never sinned, He was first of all the Son of God. He was on earth to do the works of the Father and annihilate the works of the devil. That was the Father's business.

A Right Heart

Because Jesus had a pure and obedient heart, He had a simple plan—He would just do what His Father was doing in Heaven. Jesus said, "Whatever the Father does, the Son also does" (John 5:19). He also said, "I say only what I have heard from the One who sent Me" (John 8:26).

Jesus was all set to do whatever His Father wanted, even if it wasn't easy. In John 5:30, He said, "I can do nothing on My own. I judge as God tells Me." The Prince of Peace knew He would need the Father's help. He said, "The Son can do nothing by Himself" (John 5:19). He would also need to be sold out, heart and soul, only wanting to please God. In John 8:29, Jesus said, "And the One who sent Me is with Me—He has not deserted Me. For I always do what pleases Him." Jesus had the right heart to bring God's Kingdom to earth.

A Mirror

Have you ever played Simon Says? Whatever the leader says or does, everyone else has to copy them. It's almost like looking in a mirror.

Jesus was this kind of follower during His time on earth. God's Son was close to His Father, loved His Dad like crazy, and knew God's voice perfectly. His faith eyes could see what was happening in Heaven. Jesus was just like a God mirror. That is why Jesus could say, "Anyone who has seen Me has seen the Father!" (John 14:9).

Jesus had a heart that wanted to obey, and it allowed Him to be filled with the Holy Spirit. That gave Him the power to do the Father's business and destroy the schemes of the devil. Acts 10:38 says, "God anointed Jesus of Nazareth with the Holy Spirit and with power. Then Jesus went around doing good and healing all who were oppressed by the devil, for God was with Him."

Right now, Jesus still shows us what our heavenly Dad is like. By being filled with the same Holy Spirit who was on Him, you can show others the Father's heart, do the works of the Father, and destroy the devil's plans.

The Father's Heart

The religious leaders during Jesus' time spent their whole lives serving God, but they were totally out of touch with the Father's heart. They even attacked Jesus for showing them what the Father wanted to do. The leaders were too hung up on making people obey the laws and rules. They thought that's what God wanted, and that miracles had stopped happening a long time ago. When Jesus did powerful miracles and helped people, He was proving to everyone that the Father had more than rules on His heart.

The leaders, sadly, cared more about the status quo than repentance. To protect themselves, they called Jesus a liar and eventually killed Him. They weren't interested in the Father's heart; they couldn't feel God's presence. They just weren't hungry.

But you can be different. God has a plan for your life— your royal mission. But your mission is more than just jaw-dropping miracles. Miracles and healings have a bigger purpose—to show the overwhelming, beautiful, passionate, and adoring heart of the Father for people. Every miracle is an invitation to get in touch with the Father's heart. His heart and His love matter more than anything else in the whole world. Jesus' life is all about the Father's love. He's telling us a story about a heavenly Dad who is crazy about us. He's calling the heart of every person to come get to know Him.

The Rest of the Story

We can go all over the world and tell others about Jesus, and that is good. People need the Truth, and when they hear it, some will get saved. But if we don't show them the Father's heart, it's like we're only telling part of the story—without the exciting ending. When Jesus was 12, He told us to be busy doing our Father's business. To do that, we need to know what's in the heart of God. When you discover this, you'll get to show off God's power, live joyfully, and feel God's presence. Bringing God's Kingdom to earth will be the adventure of a lifetime!

Even though you may not be an adult yet, you can do this. You can bring the Kingdom to your school, church, home, or even the mall. Every person in the world is a bull's-eye waiting to be hit with God's love.

One of our young leaders, a 12-year-old girl named Serena, was in a store one day and saw a little girl. As she looked at her, Serena's spiritual x-ray vision showed her a picture of Jesus holding the little girl in His arms. Serena told her mom what she had just seen and asked, "Should I go tell her?" Serena was a bit shy and didn't go over and talk to the little girl or her mother right away. But she kept seeing them in the store, and finally, in the parking lot, Serena just went for it and told the girl's mom, "I just saw your daughter in the arms of Jesus."

The mom began to cry and said, "You don't know what that means to me. I have been so afraid. I've been having nightmares about bad things happening to my child, and now I feel she will be okay and that she is safe. Thank you so much!"

When you give away what God has given you, God's Kingdom of light comes to destroy the kingdom of darkness. As a child of the King, this is a huge privilege. It's your royal mission.

Royal Riches

So far, we've been talking about the incredible truth of who you are and what your heavenly Dad has given you. You are a:

- Royal prince or princess

- Precious child of the King

- Costly treasure

For your royal mission you have:

- The keys of power and authority

- The Holy Spirit—your friend, leader, and guide

- The presence of God Himself

- His anointing, which is the power of God, smeared all over you

- Faith that can see invisible worlds

- Prayer that can bring Heaven to earth

- The Father's heart that brings joy, power, and love to those who are hungry and hurting

Don't you feel rich? You are! Wondering if you're valuable or good enough for all this? You totally are!

As you follow God, your royal mission will go from exciting to thrilling, with more and more adventures waiting for you. Here are some tools that will help you discover even more treasure in the Kingdom.

Prayer—Talk to God. Ask Him to use you to show His Kingdom to others. Ask for miracles to happen wherever you go.

God's Word—Invite the Holy Spirit to show you things when you read God's Word. Read about Jesus and how He showed people the Kingdom of God and the Father's heart.

Read—Read books about God's heroes—those who brought God's Kingdom to earth.

Get prayed for—Ask people who are anointed and showing God's power to pray for you. You will get what they have!

Hang out with heroes—You know all about how David killed Goliath. But did you know that at least four other giants were killed by men who followed David, the first giant killer? Spend time with people who have a heart like yours. Be around those people who are doing great things with God.

Jesus said, "As the Father has sent Me, so I am sending you" (John 20:21). He did the works of the Father, and now you can do them too! In the next chapter, we're covering even more tools to help you complete your royal mission.

Time with Your King

The only way Jesus could do the Father's business was by being very close to Him. Jesus spent time listening to His Father.

He prayed and talked to Him. He was able to see the Father with His faith eyes. He could hear His Father's voice.

In a quiet place, enter into the Father's presence. Thank Him for His goodness.

Tell Him how much you love Him. Listen to what He says. Let Him show you His works. Let Him show you His heart.

Tell Him you will do whatever He shows you. Let Him know how much you need Him.

Tell Him how much you want to please your Dad.

Journal Time

1.   Write down what the Father showed you about His works.

2. Write about what the Father's heart looks like.

Mission Objectives

Ask the Holy Spirit to take you on a Kingdom adventure.

Let the Father show you someone you can pray for. Check out what the Father is doing.

Do what the Father is doing. Do what He shows you. Write what happened.

Chapter 10

NICE IS NOT ENOUGH

Having good character is critical to your success. What's character? It's how you act and behave when no one is watching. It's the type of person you are. If you have good character, you are:

- Honest—no lies, no cheating

- Kind—helpful without being asked, never mean

- Polite—respect people right off the bat

- Trustworthy—people believe what you say

- Humble—don't brag or bully

- Sharing—give what you have without requiring payment

Jesus was like this—polite, honest, kind, and humble. Many people, Christian and non-Christian alike, are impressed by good character. You're going to need it. Some people even think that good character is more important than being connected to God's power. Yeah, you should be nice, but the truth is, *nice is not enough!* The devil isn't scared of *nice*. If nice is all you have, you won't bother him in the slightest. Being nice and having good character will help you out in life, but they won't do a thing to defeat the kingdom of darkness.

Your Royal Mission

What was that royal mission again? You are here to:

- Show others the Father's heart and love.

- Do His good works—including miracles!

- Destroy the works of the devil.

- Bring Heaven to earth.

Your royal mission is to *change the world!* What did Jesus need for that kind of job? *God's power.*

You Can Have Both!

Being nice will not show the whole reality of God's Kingdom. You need God's power *and* good character. Jesus had both—so how can you have good character and God's power like Jesus? *Obey* God.

Jesus told His followers to go and teach people the best way to live. He told them to heal the sick, raise the dead, and set people free from the devil. (Read Matthew 10:8.) That's the goal for a follower of Jesus. When you obey what Jesus said, miracles start popping up all around you. That's when you start to look and act like Jesus.

Some people think they need better character before they can do miracles. Thing is, Jesus never said you need to be nice to show His power. He just told us to listen to God and obey Him.

How Do You Act?

You are a royal prince or princess. Your Dad made the entire universe. Your big brother, Jesus, is the King of all kings, the One who *beat death*. Someone like you, who rules over a kingdom, lives their life a bit differently from the rest.

As a royal child, you:

- Have courage

- Love your heavenly Father more
  than anything

- Use your power and authority to honor God

- Show others what Heaven is like

- Show good character

For all this, you're going to need the power of the Holy Spirit. Remember, kings and prophets were anointed, or smeared with oil, before they began to live out their new, powerful role. Just like them, you need the anointing of the Holy Spirit so you'll look, think, and act like Jesus.

Say a friend of yours at school is sick. You hear God whisper that He wants you to pray for that person. When you obey and pray for them, the Holy Spirit does two things. First, He will leak out of you and do the miracle. Second, He will transform you on the inside, making you more like Jesus.

Why Power?

Some people think that we only have the Holy Spirit to stop us from sinning. That might sound nice, but it just isn't true. The power of sin was already broken when Jesus died on the Cross. Jesus won, and now we have the prize—freedom from sin, and the keys of power and authority. "This means that anyone who belongs to Christ has become a new person. The old life is gone; a new life has begun!" (2 Cor. 5:17). Sin is powerless to control you, so you already don't have to sin anymore! That's what Jesus came to give us.

It would be kind of redundant if the Holy Spirit was inside us to do the same thing Jesus already did. No, God's power is for something else—the Holy Spirit helps you show everyone what Heaven is like. God's Kingdom is full of miracles, and His presence and power make those miracles happen. Guess what else you need power for. Boldness! God's power in you gives you the courage to do impossible things. No more fearing to obey God, no more being shy, and forget about nervousness! You have no worries—the devil is crushed, and you and God are here to fix the damage he's done.

Dangerous!

Your heavenly Dad made you to be *dangerous*—not just nice! Jesus was the most dangerous person on earth—just ask the devil and his kingdom of darkness! He wiped them out, and even today, the demons are still sobbing in fear when they hear His name. As soon as Jesus gave you the keys of power and authority, you became dangerous, too!

Good character is important, sure. But guess what? *You can't make yourself good.* All you can do is obey God's directions—then *He* makes you good. Jesus said, "I can do nothing on My own. I judge as God tells Me. Therefore, My judgment is just, because I carry out the will of the One who sent Me, not My own will" (John 5:30). If you're worried about whether you'll be able to follow God's directions, don't be—it's easy when you love Him.

The plan was for Jesus' followers to show everyone the Kingdom, and they needed power for that. So before Jesus went back to Heaven, He told them to wait for the Holy Spirit to come. (Look up Acts 1:4-5.) The disciples waited in a room together for days. Finally, the Holy Spirit came... with *power*. It changed them, and then they changed the world. Spirit-filled believers could teleport, jails fell apart around them, and they couldn't be killed. (Read about all this in Acts 8:39-40; 14:19-20; 16:26; and 28:3-6.) Now that's dangerous!

God's presence is where character and power come from. If you hang out in the sun, you'll get a tan—or maybe a sunburn! Either way, the sun changes your skin color, and you can end up looking quite different if you change enough. The presence of God is like the sun—it'll tan you to His color!

A Friend of God

Do you ever want to hurt your friends? I hope not! How about the Holy Spirit? Do you want to hurt Him? The Holy Spirit is an amazing friend—the best you'll ever have. The Bible says, "And do not bring sorrow to God's Holy Spirit by the way you live" (Eph. 4:30). How can you hurt Him in the way you live? Sin, plain and simple. When you choose to do wrong or choose *not* to do right, it hurts God's Holy Spirit. That's no way to treat your best friend.

Another thing the Bible says is, "Do not stifle the Holy Spirit" (1 Thess. 5:19). That means don't "stop the flow." Remember—the Holy Spirit is leaking out of you. *Let Him.* He is ready to bring people to you so they can be saved, healed, and set free from the devil. He wants you to let His power flow through you to these people. That's being friends with the Holy Spirit—working together!

This is what God wants every single day to look like. How do you get to that point? By just wanting more and more of

Him. God wants you to be hungry for His power and presence. What does hunger look like? Let's say you know someone who is doing powerful things with God. You want to do what they are doing. Just ask that person to pray for you, and your Father will give you the same anointing. One of the best prayers you can ever say is, "More, Lord—I want more of You."

Now Do It!

So when God gives you more of Himself and His power, what do you do? Give it away! In God's Kingdom, you can only keep what you give away. Look for those who are sick and ask if you can pray for them. You are not the healer, but you can give them the Healer—God!

Jesus came to earth to show the Father's heart and love for people. Only someone with the power of the Holy Spirit could do it. You can never have too much of His power or character. Remember who you are, and what you get to do. God does not want you to have just a nice, quiet life. Nice is not enough! Be *dangerous!*

So far we have been discovering who you are, what you have, and what you get to do. And here's how you bring God's Kingdom to earth:

* Look—use your spiritual x-ray vision to see what your heavenly Father is doing.

* Listen—with your heart to what God is saying.

- Obey—what the Holy Spirit wants you to do.

Your Father has lots more for you. He loves prepping you for your royal mission!

Time with Your King

Ask your heavenly Dad to come. Let the Holy Spirit bring you into His presence. Tell Dad how great He is.

Tell Him how much you love Him. Let the Father love on you for a while.

Ask Him to show you again who you are. You will see what He sees—a Royal Child. Take a good look.

In His presence, ask Jesus to give you what He has. Tell Him you want to be just like Him.

Thank Him for His power. Thank Him that you don't have to sin anymore. Thank Him for His courage. Thank Him for His love.

Let Dad know you want to obey Him. Let Him know you are hungry. Be ready to receive His power and character.

Journal Time

1. Write about what the Father showed you.

2. What does He see when He looks at you?

3. What does a royal child look like?

4.   What did Jesus do when you told Him you want to be just like Him?

5.   What did you get from the Father when you said you want to obey Him?

6.   What does His power and character look like?

Mission Objectives

God wants you to have good character and be dangerous. Good character comes when you are hungry for Him and want to obey.

Look for someone who is sick or needs prayer. Ask if you can pray for them. Let the Holy Spirit help you. Let Him leak out of you. Write what happened.

Is there someone you know who is doing powerful things with God? Ask them if they would pray for you. Thank them.

Write what you received.

Chapter 11

FOLLOW THE SIGNS

It was a Sunday morning. We were in a church in a small African village. As the service was ending, about 25 women and children came to the front for prayer. Our team began to pray. One by one, everyone was healed of sickness and pain. We all saw God's presence and power shining bright!

Later that day, one boy came to our hut. He asked if we would come and pray for his father to be healed. We went to his home and prayed for his father. Right away God's power touched him, and he felt a little better. The next day the boy's father came by and asked if we would pray some more. As we prayed, God healed him!

We could see with our spiritual vision that something was happening to the man's heart, too. We asked if he would like to meet the One who healed him, Jesus, and he said yes. He became a Christian that day. We were so excited about what God had done!

This man had been the leader of the young men in the village. He and the others did not like Christians. When Christian doctors would come to his village, he would cut down thorn bushes and put them on the road so it was hard for people to get through. He didn't want Christians anywhere near him. But when Jesus came into his heart, this man changed completely. He was now our friend. He loved Christians, and he loved God. Everywhere we went, he went with us. He even gave us his best goat!

What happened? What made this man so hungry for prayer? His son, the one who brought us to him, had been extremely sick just that morning—until God healed him. When the father saw his son healed, it got his attention. Then, when God healed the father's sickness, it was a sign of His power and love. That made the father want something even greater than healing—God Himself! That's why he asked Jesus to come into his heart. That's where the real change happened.

Signs, Signs, Signs

Revival is what happens when God's power explodes onto the scene, Heaven comes to earth, and people see God's Kingdom. Revival brings change. People repent and abandon their past sins. People who love God can bring Him into schools, churches, restaurants, malls, and homes. Whole cities and even countries can turn to God as people begin to see with faith. Peace, healing, and joy come and kick out the kingdom of darkness, hatred, sickness, and fear. God's Kingdom of light rules in a revival.

Signs and wonders help make revival happen as people see miracles. They get a firsthand look at God's presence and power, and suddenly, they can't ignore Him anymore.

Before you can get your driver's license, chances are you'll have to pass a test that proves you recognize all the different road signs and understand what they mean. Signs like these are everywhere in our world, and they're extremely helpful and important. Without them, no one would be safe on the roads.

Have you ever taken a road trip to somewhere awesome? Where did you go? If it was a long trip, maybe you remember the first time you saw a sign for your destination and knew you were close. "New York City: 60 miles," "Welcome to Disneyland"—pretty exciting, right? You might even whip out the camera and take a picture of the sign. But did you even think about stopping and staying at the sign? Not likely! Why? Because the sign wasn't the destination. It was pointing to something even better, and it was exciting, but if you decided to hang out by the sign itself, you'd miss out on all the fun!

When you think of a miraculous healing, or even someone being raised from the dead, did it ever occur to you that those signs, wonders, and miracles are just like that road sign? They help us get to our revival—they point the way to something even greater. But God's signs—even the most exciting ones—aren't the best part. What's the best part? Well, let's follow the signs and see where they take us.

Signs and Wonders Show What God Is Like

You are here to be a witness for God—that means you show what God is like, and that includes God's power. God isn't helpless and hopeless in the face of sickness, death, blind eyes, and deaf ears. Miracles show us what He's *really* like. He's like sickness vanishing and leaving you feeling like a million bucks. He's like the deaf person being able to listen to music again, like the once-blind person now watching the sun rise. He's like *life* instead of death.

Without miracles, people won't get to see this side of God. They will miss out on knowing that His powerful love can and will take care of them—because that's how much He cares.

Signs and Wonders Help People Choose Right or Wrong

Luke 5 tells the story of how Peter was recruited as Jesus' disciple. He had been fishing all night long without catching anything. Jesus stepped into his boat and asked him to row out a bit, giving Him a handy platform to preach from. After the message, He told Peter to throw out his net and give it one more shot. There were no fish around, so it seemed like a dumb idea, but Peter obeyed anyway. The next thing he knew, he had so many fish in his net that it nearly sank his boat.

Peter saw this as a sign of God's power and said, "Oh, Lord, please leave me—I'm too much of a sinner to be around You" (Luke 5:8). Jesus didn't have to tell Peter that. Miracles are just like a light that turns on and shows us what's in our hearts. In the face of signs and wonders, it's easy to see the sin in our lives and repent.

There are, however, some people who choose not to follow God, even when they see miracles. Pharaoh, the king of Egypt, turned against the Hebrews when he saw the signs and wonders of the ten plagues. The Bible says his heart was hard. (Read Exodus 9:35.) The religious leaders also turned against Jesus even after they saw all of His great miracles. They refused to repent. When people see signs and wonders, they will make a choice—either to come to God's love or to reject Him.

Signs and Wonders Give Us Courage

It's hugely important that we tell others about the miracles God has done and is doing—these are our testimonies, and they're made for sharing. Why do we have to keep repeating stories we've already heard? Because our memories are short! Think about it—would you remember all your friends' birthdays without Facebook reminding you? Maybe, maybe not, but the reminder sure helps you plan the party! Sharing testimonies reminds us how amazing our heavenly Dad is and how special we are as sons and daughters of the King. Remembering how God's power destroys the works of the devil gives us courage to bravely face down the enemy.

In the Old Testament, there was a group of brave warriors—the sons of Ephraim. They were powerful fighters, but on the day the battle started, they panicked and ran. Why? The Bible says, "They did not keep God's covenant and refused to live by His instructions. They forgot what He had done—the great wonders He had shown them, the miracles He did for their ancestors" (Ps. 78:10-12). When the sons of Ephraim forgot how powerful their God was, they forgot who they were. They lost their courage to fight and win the battle.

Miracles Show God's Glory

In John 2, Jesus attended a wedding. Disaster struck when they ran out of wine. (Can you imagine a wedding reception with no cake? It was that much of a problem.) Jesus had not done any miracles yet, but His mother, Mary, knew who her Son was. Mary told Jesus:

> *"They have no more wine."*
>
> *"Dear woman, that's not our problem," Jesus replied. "My time has not yet come."*
>
> *But His mother told the servants, "Do whatever He tells you"* (John 2:3-5).

Remember, Jesus only did what He saw His Father doing in Heaven. If He didn't turn the water into wine at first, it was because He didn't see His Father doing it. But when Mary used her faith and told everyone to do what her Son said, something happened in Heaven. Jesus took another look at His Father, and God was turning water into wine.

Mary's faith changed Heaven! Now was the time for Jesus to be glorified. Jesus' first miracle happened because of His mom's faith, and when miracles happen, God gets the glory. His power pushes away satan's kingdom of darkness with the light of God's presence. The glory of God makes darkness disappear, and God's Kingdom of light takes its place. The Kingdom of Heaven rules—and you get to do this too! You can bring God's Kingdom of light and glory into the darkness.

Signs Help People Give Glory to God

Matthew 9:8 says that when the people saw the man healed, they glorified God. The man in this story could not move—until Jesus met him and forgave his sins. Then He told the man to get up and walk, and he did. Seriously impressed, the people started to praise God and give Him glory.

When signs, wonders, and miracles happen, it gets people's attention. When they watch as God's power destroys the works of the devil, something happens inside of them. Their hearts open wide, and they start to praise! It's like the way you feel when your favorite sports team wins, only better! The more God stories you hear, the more your heart will praise and glorify your Father. Yay God!

Signs and Wonders Reveal Jesus

Jesus was trying to tell the Jews that He was their Savior, but many did not believe Him. Then He said, "But if I do His work, believe in the evidence of the miraculous works I have done, even if you don't believe Me. Then you will know and understand that the Father is in Me, and I am in the Father" (John 10:38). Jesus knew that if people would just believe in the concrete signs of His miracles, they would find their way to Him. Miracles reveal who Jesus really is.

Miracles Help People Hear God's Voice

Most people in their everyday lives don't spend a lot of time thinking about Heaven. They have too many earthly things to worry about. But when these people hear testimonies of God's power, their hearts turn toward Heaven. They start to take a serious look at God's invisible Kingdom, and Heaven starts to look a little more real and relevant. When Heaven looks and feels real, people realize that they need to repent and get serious with God. Miracles also make people hungry for God, because they show what a good God He is. People get hungry when they get a taste of God's goodness. They want more, the ears of their hearts open, and they start to listen. That's when they can finally hear what the Father has to say to them.

Miracles Reveal Jesus and His Church

The Bible says Jesus is the head, or leader, of the church. (Read Ephesians 5:23.) We are His followers. We are called His Body, the Church. (Read 1 Corinthians 12:27.) Your head doesn't have any plans to cut itself off and leave your body, right? Let's hope not! The head and the body stick together—things work out better that way for both of them. Jesus, as the Head of the Church, made a promise to you, His Body—He will *never* leave you.

God's presence comforts us and brings us close to Him. His presence also gives us courage to show His great power and love. Miracles prove that God Himself is with you. They help you complete your royal mission—to bring Heaven to earth.

Signs and wonders are key. They point to something greater—God Himself! Signs help us get from where we are to the new places the Holy Spirit wants to take us. He has some crazy adventures for you in His Kingdom. His presence and power will lead you—just follow the signs.

Time with Your King

Invite God's presence. Thank Him for who He is. Thank Him for His kindness, care, and His power. Thank Him for being such a loving Dad.

Ask the Father what revival looks like. Let Him show you what He sees when He looks at your school, church, home, or mall.

Ask Him for His Kingdom to come to those places. Ask Him for signs and wonders. Ask Him for revival.

Let Him show you His glory. Ask Him to use you.

Journal Time

1.   Write down what revival would look like where you live.

2.   What does God's glory look like?

3.   Search through your Bible and find at least three signs, wonders, or miracles.

Mission Objectives

Begin to pray for revival, signs, and wonders in your:

- school

- church

- home

- mall

Start using your spiritual x-ray vision when you go to these places. Pray what you see in the Spirit.

Share testimonies or God stories with your family at home.

Share with your friends at school, youth group, and when you're hanging out together.

Write what happens.

Chapter 12

TREASURE FOR EVERYONE

God made a vow to you when He said, "I am with you always" (Matt. 28:20). Because of that, you can rely on His great love—and He loves being with you! God's presence is not only a love gift, but it is also the source of courage. You are definitely going to need courage to complete your royal mission as an ambassador, bringing Heaven to earth and defeating satan. It takes courage to change the world!

God's presence is more valuable than anything on earth—and He lives in your heart! In a sense, that makes your heart the ultimate treasure chest. You're a lot like some of these heroes in the Bible—treasure-bearers who changed the world:

- Apostle Paul preached the gospel to many people.

- King David ruled a nation.

- Moses led the Hebrews out of Egypt and slavery.

- Gideon led the Israelites into victory against great enemies.

Jesus told His followers to go into the world to preach the gospel and do miracles. They were not perfect people. But Jesus asked them to change the world, and they did! It happened because Jesus said, "I will be with you." He's with you too!

Carrying His Presence

Everyone who is a Christian has this promise of God's presence. So, how do you carry His presence with you? It happens when you:

- Know that you have a great treasure inside of you.

- Spend time loving Dad each day.

- Talk, act, and have attitudes that please the Holy Spirit.

- Are careful to not make the Holy Spirit feel bad.

- Want to put God first in everything.

Try walking with God this way and you will let the Holy Spirit do powerful things. Your ordinary life will be full of daily adventures.

The anointing displays God's presence in you. You are *smeared* and covered with God's power-filled presence. Miracles just start happening when you walk by, covered with and leaking the Holy Spirit. The anointing isn't made to be kept to yourself—God wants you to spread it around. Don't hide the treasure inside you! Remember, in the Kingdom of God you only get to keep what you give away.

Spread Him Around

Your heavenly Dad has given you so much that you just have to share with others. Open up your treasure chest filled with God's presence and give Him away to those who are hungry for the Father. God wants you to give them a chance to see, hear, and feel His presence, because meeting God is what changes lives.

God's anointing on you is what makes it possible for others to meet God through you. Have you ever had glitter on you, or handled something covered in glitter, like a Christmas decoration? (Guys, no shame if you have. Real men aren't scared of glitter.) That stuff is tricky! Whatever you put it on will never be glitter-free after that, no matter how much you wash it off! And the minute you touch glitter, it's sticking all over you! What would happen if you got glitter-bombed—so now you're sparkling like a diamond mine—and then started bumping up against all your friends, giving out free hugs? You'd be glitter-contagious in the worst way! Everyone would be sparkling pretty soon!

In the same way, when you are smeared with God's presence, the Holy Spirit sticks to everyone you touch. You shed Him wherever you walk! When He rubs off on others, guess what happens? People get healed, fear and hatred leave, and demons run away screaming. The anointing breaks the chains that satan puts on people.

God rubs off a lot when you share His Word and pray for people. But there are other ways to spread the glitter of the Holy Spirit. It can happen all the time! Lives can change just because you and God walk into a room together. It's like doing a cannonball into the pool. What happens? There is a huge splash, and the water goes flying outward to soak anyone standing too close. When you go to school, to the mall, or anywhere, you can make a big splash, too. You and God's presence can blast away the kingdom of darkness and soak people with His power!

Jesus said you can even leave His peace wherever you go. The people around you might feel different after you leave, if you were giving away God's presence. The devil and the kingdom of darkness will scatter, leaving a fresh, peaceful feeling in the air. The demons are terrified of you because of what you carry—God's presence.

Jesus Takes a Walk

One day Jesus went for a walk—and, as usual, a huge crowd gathered around Him. Everyone was pushing and shoving to be close to Him. In the midst of this huge crowd, there was a woman who had an incurable sickness. She reached out and touched just the edge of Jesus' robe. Suddenly, Jesus stopped and asked, "Who touched My robe?" (Mark 5:30). His disciples were surprised and thought, *Good grief, Jesus. Everyone touched You. Just look at this crowd!* But Jesus said He felt power flow out of Him. The anointing of the Holy Spirit that was on Jesus rubbed off onto the sick woman. Her faith got the Holy Spirit to leak out of Him and break the chains of sickness that the devil had cursed her with. She was now healed and free!

You have the same Holy Spirit anointing and power that Jesus had. Listen and He will tell you when you can pour out God's presence. Just let the Holy Spirit do what He wants to do, and miracles will happen. Let God smear you with Himself!

If you were carrying around a bag of sandwiches and met a group of starving people, wouldn't you share? They're dying without food, and you have more than you need. You'd probably share, right? It's just like that with God's presence—you've got it, people need it, and your Father wants everybody to have it. So share it! Be filled with God's Holy Spirit so that you have lots to give. Only a full water balloon can get anyone wet! God just loves to pour out His Spirit on you and splash all over everyone you meet. It delights Him when you overflow and leak His Spirit. He never runs out of promises. So get filled over and over again!

Amazing Angels

Angels are amazing creatures. They are powerful and full of glory. Angels spend their free time in Heaven worshiping God. In the Bible, whenever angels came to earth people would freak out and start worshiping them. Of course, we're not supposed to worship angels—as the angels keep reminding us—but we do need to know what they are here to do. Angels are sent to earth to help us show others God's Kingdom. We need a little angel help from time to time as we bring Heaven to earth.

Most angels are bored! Why? Because they are waiting around for people like you to step up and do impossible things, like miracles. Angels are impatient to help you in your royal mission, and they get pumped and love to be around guys and girls who are *dangerous*. Being dangerous keeps angels busy! They will always follow those who walk by faith with the Holy Spirit and use their spiritual x-ray vision. They will protect you from any attack and help others receive from God. These messengers from Heaven want to help you spread the Kingdom.

Sent from Heaven

As you go on your journey to complete your royal mission, remember that angels are ready and waiting to help you do amazing and exciting things. How do you get them involved? The Bible says that angels are sent when people pray. They come to help answer your prayers.

You are from another world. You are a royal child of the King. Wherever you go, you bring an open Heaven with you. What's that? It means you are like a gate or ladder to Heaven. Wherever you are, angels will come too, and God will send anything in Heaven that you need to show His love and power to people. Heaven will follow you.

Angels also listen for God's voice and word. They will go and do whatever the Father says. When you echo the Father's heart, guess what happens? Angels listen! When you sound just like God, they come down from Heaven to make sure that what you prayed about will happen. That is why you can pray with boldness. You don't have to be shy. You have the keys of power and authority. The angels are listening! They are pumped about helping you give away your treasure!

Surprises!

One Sunday morning, I was teaching in children's church. Suddenly, there was an explosion of colored feathers in the air! A second later, *poof*, more feathers appeared out of nowhere. As the green, yellow, red, and purple feathers floated to the floor, the kids jumped up and climbed over the chairs to catch them. Everybody was laughing with joy at this sign and wonder!

There are many things we can watch for that will let us know God just showed up. Sometimes people will fall on the floor. Sometimes they will start laughing. (God likes to tickle His kids.) I have seen oil and gold dust cover the hands of youth and adults. We have even smelled and tasted God's presence in our classroom!

Your Father is a big fan of surprises. He doesn't like to hide in a plain, boring box. He's into doing new and different things, just to make your jaw drop and your eyes pop. With every sign or surprise, we discover how amazing our heavenly Dad is. He has a lot more surprises to show you! Keep following the signs—you will discover that there is treasure for everyone!

In the next chapter, we're getting into another cool topic—what it means to be like Jesus.

Time with Your King

Ask the Holy Spirit to take you into the presence of the Father.

Thank your Papa for His promise to be with you. Thank Him for His love gift.

Tell Him how much you like to be with Him. Thank your Father for the treasure that is in your heart.

Thank Him that you get to carry His presence. Let the Holy Spirit smear you with Himself.

Tell Him you want to give your great treasure away to hungry people.

Ask the Father to show you His angels.

Journal Time

1.   Write down what the treasure in your heart looks like.

2.   What is it like to be smeared with God, the Holy Spirit?

3.   Write about the angels God has shown you.

Mission Objectives

Ask the Holy Spirit to lead you to a place where He could rub off on someone.

Wherever you go, pray for God's peace and Kingdom to come.

Look for someone you can give your treasure to.

Let the Holy Spirit leak out at your school, wherever you hang out, and at your home.

Write about all the things that happened.

Chapter 13

JUST LIKE JESUS

Jesus! When you hear or see that name, what comes to mind? What images, sounds, or words do you think of?

One day the apostle John saw Jesus in a vision. John saw Jesus with hair as white as snow. His eyes were like flames of fire. His feet shone like polished metal. When John heard Jesus' voice, it thundered like a loud waterfall. (Read Revelation 1:13-16.)

The truth is, Jesus is in Heaven right now. He's sitting on a throne right next to the Father. His glory is beyond anything we could imagine. Angels and heavenly creatures worship Him nonstop. Jesus has won the victory, and all His enemies are now groveling at His feet.

You desperately need to see Jesus. You absolutely *must* know what He is like today. Why? Because the Bible says, "As He [Jesus] is, so also are we in this world" (1 John 4:17 NKJV).

The Bible says you are just like Jesus is right now. Does that sound impossible? Well, if you had to manage it by yourself, it would be. But God, the Holy Spirit, takes care of this for you because He adores you. He comforts you, He gives you gifts, and He covers you with His power. His ultimate goal is to make you just like Jesus.

An artist setting out to create a masterpiece will often set up a model to observe and work from. That is what the Holy Spirit does with you. He is the artist, you are the artwork, and Jesus is the model.

When Jesus went back to Heaven, He became the perfect model. He is full of glory, full of power, full of victory. Now the artist, the Holy Spirit, is here to make us His masterpiece—a beautiful painting that looks exactly like Jesus!

The Cross

We must never forget what Jesus did on the Cross—it's too vital to our lives. The Cross reminds us how incredibly huge God's love for us is. It's proof that the wonderful blood of Jesus destroyed all the power of sin in our lives forever. The Cross means we can be one of God's royal children. But the Cross is just the beginning of what it means to be a Christian.

Jesus isn't on the Cross now! He rose from the dead, and now He's alive! That's our Jesus today. His power over sin and death gives you the power to be a royal ruler!

Some people are still miserable and grieving because Jesus had to die on the Cross. Jesus doesn't want you to spend eternity apologizing for making Him go through that; He wants you to thank Him for what He did! When Jesus was beaten and died on the Cross:

- He became poor so you could be rich.

- He was whipped and hurt so you could be healed and well.

- He took your sin so you could be forgiven and free from sin.

Jesus became like the people in the world—poor, sick, and full of sin—so we could become like Him! We can be like He is *now*. You could never repay the Father for what Jesus did. The best thing you can do to honor and thank Jesus is to make His sacrifice count and become just like Him.

Look Up, Not In

Remember when Jesus said, "the Son can do nothing by Himself" (John 5:19)? He knew He was just a man. He couldn't do any miracles by Himself. Did that make Jesus miserable? Did He walk around wallowing in self-pity? Did He look in the mirror and think He was just a weakling? Nope! Jesus just looked up at His Father in Heaven, followed the Holy Spirit, and let God leak out of Him.

Some people forget what Jesus did for them. They might look at themselves and see all their weaknesses. They might talk about how awful they used to be, if they keep thinking about their old sins even after the Father has forgiven them. These thoughts are just tricks and lies of the devil. Your Father doesn't want you to be obsessed with criticizing yourself. Royal rulers don't look at themselves—they look up to their King. That's what Jesus did. Jesus depended on His Father and changed the world. You can too!

The Holy Spirit made you like Jesus. You are priceless. Because your heavenly Dad is beyond rich and massively powerful, you don't have to moan and groan about being weak. Don't agree with satan's lies. The devil likes to say you can't do anything right, you're dumb, or you're weak—don't agree with him! Agree with God and shout, "I can do everything through Christ, who gives me strength" (Phil. 4:13)!

Say that out loud so you can hear it with your ears. It helps to hear yourself agreeing with God. Use that spiritual x-ray vision, and add your voice on top of that. See what your Father sees in you, and then agree. When you do that, you rake in the blessings. The Father showers you with good stuff. You feel closer to Him than ever. This blesses God, too. When you declare who you truly are, what you are really saying is that God did a fantastic job in making you, loving you, and saving you! Your Father doesn't get any credit when you put yourself down.

Being Like Him

The Bible says that as Jesus is, so are we in this world (look up 1 John 4:17). Jesus is sitting on a throne in Heaven.

He is awesome and wonderful, full of glory, full of power, He has won the victory, and He is holy. This is who Jesus is. He wants you to have all of that. Let's talk about four things that Jesus wants to give you. He wants you to show these things to others so they can see His Kingdom on earth.

Glory

Jesus lives inside everyone who has been saved and forgiven of sin. But the glory of God seems to rest on certain people. When the glory and presence of Jesus is on someone, it's bright like sunshine or a burning fire. When Jesus' disciples were filled with the baptism of the Holy Spirit, there were flames of fire over each person's head. No one could explain it, but it was the glory of God that came crashing into that room.

Even today we sometimes see fire when God's presence is especially powerful on people. Satan and his kingdom of darkness cannot put this fire out—all he can do is duck and cover. Jesus said He is coming back for a Church full of royal rulers who are full of His glory. Ask Him for His glory to come rest on you.

Power

As Jesus sits on His throne, power streams out from Him in a nonstop flood. If you're like Him, you will radiate His power, too. The baptism of the Holy Spirit puts you into a "super suit." If a cape-wearing superhero is walking down your street, do you think people will notice? Yup! And people will also notice your super suit—the Holy Spirit. They can't miss His power when they see the miracles and feel God's presence on you.

The Bible says that the power of God:

- Saves people

- Heals sick and hurting bodies

- Takes away fear, misery, and depression

- Forgives you and adopts you as a child of God

- Lets our immortal spirits live with God, our Dad

Show off the power of Jesus, and show the world the Kingdom of Heaven!

Victory

Jesus utterly wrecked His enemies. He destroyed the powers of darkness and hell. He trashed death, sin, and the works of the devil. Jesus rose from the dead and sits next to His Father, surrounded in glory. Everything that has a name is at His feet, every power in the world has to submit to Him. He won the victory, He has the keys, and now you do too!

You've probably seen the Super Bowl, right? Maybe you watched the game and rooted for your team, or maybe you just wanted to see the commercials. Either way, one team wins in the end—there's confetti everywhere, bright lights, and the Lombardi trophy. How do the winners look? Pretty happy? Those guys have some of the biggest smiles on their faces that you'll ever see on TV! They may have lost some games during the season, but they aren't acting like losers now! They're winners, and they've got the joy to prove it.

This is how God wants you to live—like a winner. The Bible says that you are *more* than a winner in Jesus. (Read Romans 8:37.) You are more than a winner because you did not even have to get into the fight. Jesus beat the devil, gave you His trophy, and handed over the keys of power and authority. You get the prize He won.

Of course, the devil is a sore loser, and he'll still want to put up a fight. He can't stand the idea of you completing your royal mission and bringing Heaven to earth. But you don't have worry about anything the kingdom of darkness tries to throw at you. You'll win every time, because you are a winner.

Holy

Jesus is perfect and holy. Everything evil is so far away from Him, it's in another dimension. Everything pure and perfect and beautiful and *good* is all around Him. That's where you are—close to Him. Being holy is not just about how you act, whether you obey the rules, or the things you can and can't do. The Bible talks about the *beauty* of holiness.

Holiness is something that radiates out of your love for God. It shines from within as you thank Jesus for what He did and follow your friend, the Holy Spirit, wherever He leads. When you show God's power, people see God's heart. When you show God's holiness, people see God's beauty.

When you know who you are in this world, you will look and walk like Jesus. People will see His Kingdom. People will see Heaven come to earth. God's love, beauty, and power will show up, and revival will sweep the world! You will complete your royal mission.

Time with Your King

As you come into the presence of your Father, thank Him for what He has given you. Thank Him for who you are.

Ask the Father to show you His Son, Jesus. What does He look like? What is He doing? What is He saying?

Come closer to King Jesus. Ask Him for His Glory. Ask Him for His power. Receive His power.

He will make you feel like a winner. He will give you His holiness. Thank Him and love on Him.

Journal Time

1. Write about what Jesus looks like.

2. What was it like to receive Jesus' glory, power, victory, and holiness?

3. Describe yourself. Do you look like Jesus?

Mission Objectives

After spending some time in the presence of your Dad, look for ways you can show others God's Kingdom.

Pray for someone who is sick or hurting.

Walk around your school or mall and ask for God's Kingdom to come.

Pray for your teachers.

Pray for your friends.

Write what happened.

Chapter 14

CLIMBING MOUNTAINS

Every week we would take teams of youth, go to different schools, and share about God's love and His Kingdom. The students we talked with learned about God and His overwhelming love. Many teens made a commitment to Jesus and were healed by God's touch. But that was just the beginning.

As God's love and power came to the classrooms and miracles happened, something else came—God's Kingdom. The students started to act differently. Teachers began to notice that the students were listening to them. People felt peace filling and surrounding the school as the students were being accepting and kind to each other. Some of the students chose God's love as the subject for their class writing assignments!

When Heaven comes to earth and touches a place like a school, home, or mall, things change in a big way. The kingdom of darkness is shoved out. God's healing love and peace sweep in. Sin, sickness, hatred, and prejudice leave.

Salt and Light

Jesus said some interesting things about you in Matthew 5:13-16. He called you salt and light. Why would He say that? Salt and light are both powerful for such simple things. Salt totally changes the flavor of food. Ever had unsalted chips or nuts? *Way* different! Salt has also been used for centuries to keep food from spoiling. Then there's light. Whenever a light is turned on, darkness is just gone. In other words, salt and light both change their surroundings. That is the way your heavenly Dad looks at you, His Church, and His Kingdom. You get to change whatever is around you!

The Father is always thinking about you, planning great and powerful adventures for your life. You are the son or daughter He loves dearly. God wants you to bring His Kingdom into the place you live and wherever you go, changing everything. Every time you spread around God's love and people meet Jesus through you, the kingdom of darkness shrivels up a little more. Every time you pray for someone and a miracle happens, the works of the devil are crushed. When you ask God to touch a person, you become a part of what changed their life. God is delighted with you when you do the same things Jesus did when He was on earth— and even greater things than that! (Read John 14:12.)

He loves to put His light—you—in dark places so His glory, love, and power will shine! Isaiah 60:2 says, "Darkness as black as night covers all the nations of the earth, but the glory of the Lord rises and appears over you."

The Mountains

So where does God want to take you on your royal mission to spread His Kingdom? Let's start with the mountains. There are many different parts to your life; we can think of them as "mountains." What are some of the mountains in your life?

Your school is one. Your church is another. Your family, and don't forget your close friends. Where you hang out, shop, or do extra-curricular activities—clubs, music, sports, arts. The movies and TV shows you spend time watching. The people around you—both rich and poor. The peace and friendship or fighting and drama in your life. The sick or healthy people you know.

These areas of life, or mountains, are very important to God and His Kingdom of Heaven. They are also important to the devil and his kingdom of darkness. The kingdom which rules these mountains (or areas of life) rules over the lives of people.

If the kingdom of darkness rules:

- Schools and malls and other hangouts are not safe.

- Families are unhappy.

- Evil, sin-filled shows and movies are made.

- People are poor and sick.

- There is no peace, only brutal wars.

If the Kingdom of Heaven rules on these mountains:

- Schools are safe and teach godly truths.

- Malls and other hangouts are safe.

- Churches are full of God's presence and power.

- Families are happy and stay together.

- Godly movies and TV shows are made.

- People are healthy and not struggling to survive.

- There is peace.

A Famous Mountain Climber

Your Father has been helping you prep for your royal mission to bring His Kingdom to earth. This journey is leading you to the mountains. If you've never climbed a mountain and aren't sure how to do it, that's okay. Your heavenly Dad is about to show you.

Some of the greatest heroes in the Bible were teenagers. God would put them in the midst of dark and difficult places so that His light would shine. They learned how to climb the mountains and change nations!

One of these heroes was a guy named Daniel. He was just a teenager when he was captured and taken away from his family, his home, his town, his country—everything. He ended up in a foreign land where they didn't even speak his language. But God stuck by him, and Daniel did the best he could in a new, foreign school. When the king heard that Daniel was a bright young man full of unusual wisdom, he brought him into his court. Soon, Daniel rose through the ranks to become the king's best advisor because of his wisdom, power, and trustworthiness. (Read Daniel 1–4.)

If Daniel makes you think mountain climbing looks easy, don't bet on it. The country that Daniel lived in was one of the darkest, most sinful places on earth. He was surrounded by evil magicians. The wicked king forced everyone into sick idol worship, and satan's kingdom was in full swing. Even though Daniel was taken away from his parents and had to live in an ungodly place full of temptation, he was not angry at God. Daniel loved God and chose to follow Him anywhere, no matter what. Daniel knew his royal mission.

Because he loved and served God faithfully, God protected Daniel from the twisted world around him. He was so close to God's goodness, love, and power that sin could not taint God's holiness in Daniel's heart.

One night the king had a weird dream. He called for all of his advisors and magicians to tell him what the dream was and what it meant. Nobody knew what the dream was about, so the king declared that they would be executed.

Daniel quickly got an audience with the king. He had insider information from God, and he told the king what the dream meant. He also told the king that the reason he knew the secret of the dream wasn't because he was wiser than the other advisors, but because God wanted them to live. The king spared the lives of all the wise men, including Daniel and his friends. Daniel did not brag about his gifts or his great wisdom. He just talked about God's greatness and goodness. He was humble.

God helped Daniel climb the mountains as a servant to the king. It did not matter that the king was evil—the important thing was that Daniel was being a servant. When you choose to serve others, even if they don't deserve it, it's like getting under them and lifting them up. God sees what you are doing, and as you serve others He'll come and lift you up as well. God will bless you as He changes the hearts of those you serve. That is why Jesus said, "Whoever wants to be first must take last place and be the servant of everyone else" (Mark 9:35).

Another Dream

The king had another dream. This one was clearly showing some impending doom for the king—a punishment for all his evil actions. Once again, Daniel knew what everything meant. But did Daniel secretly feel relieved that the king was going to get what he deserved? No, Daniel was just as upset as the king. He wished it was for the king's enemies, instead, because Daniel was loyal to the king and wanted the best for him. Daniel honored the king—not because of anything the king had done, but because he honored God and his royal mission.

Daniel was God's special agent, just like you. He was able to infiltrate the enemy's kingdom of darkness. When he became a servant of the king, he brought God's light with him, and darkness fled. The king's sinful heart changed. He said, "Now I, Nebuchadnezzar, praise and glorify and honor the King of heaven. All His acts are just and true, and He is able to humble the proud" (Dan. 4:37). The king was saved! The most evil kingdom on earth was touched by Heaven! An entire nation turned to God! Satan lost because Daniel climbed to the top of the mountain!

Gather Your Stuff

If you want to go on a hike in the woods, you'd get ready by gathering all the things you're going to need. You'd probably pack them in a backpack. So, what are you going to take for your journey to the mountains, to the different parts of your life? What will go into your backpack? What has your Dad given you for this exciting adventure?

Keys of Power and Authority: This is the trophy and prize Jesus won for you. As a royal ruler, you have Father God's power and authority.

Spiritual x-ray vision: This is your heart's vision. You will be able to see the unseen worlds of God's Kingdom and the kingdom of darkness. You will also see what the Father is doing in Heaven, just like Jesus did.

Prayer: This brings lightning down from Heaven. It will let loose Heaven's blessings and lock up the evil things that are on earth.

Grace: This is God's promise to give you all the help you will need to complete your royal mission.

God's presence: You will have the promise of the Father's love, peace, courage, and protection. The strength of His joy will be a great help. With God's presence you will have no fear of the enemy or other people's opinions of you.

A mirror: God will show you that you are just like His Son, Jesus. You are more than a winner. You have His glory and power.

Angels: As you speak the same words that are in the Father's heart, angels will rise up to help bring Heaven to earth.

God stories: Sharing stories about God's love and power will do amazing things. It will open people's hearts and make them hungry for the Father's goodness.

Not only do you have all these great things to take along on your mission, but you also have a Guide, a best Friend, the *Holy Spirit*.

You will be smeared with the anointing of the Holy Spirit. God's power and love will rub off on people you touch. You'll leak the Holy Spirit wherever you go. His presence and power will flow out of you to do "impossible" things like miracles. These signs and wonders will point the way to God's love and goodness.

You'll get to be filled and refilled with God's love and joy. As you soak in His presence, it will be like a drink of cool water on a blistering hot day. It'll help you stay fresh and strong on your journey.

Your spirit will speak in tongues—your special language to God. Doing so will bless Him and make your spirit grow stronger each day.

Your Backpack

As you can see, you're kitted out with stuff to pack into your backpack! But how about that backpack itself? It's special too—it's going to carry all those awesome gifts and promises.

Your backpack is your heart, and it's the last thing you want to forget to take with you on your royal mission. You need it the most! Daniel had the perfect heart, or backpack. His heart:

- Was humble—he gave God all the glory for the things that happened.

- Wanted to serve God and the king.

- Was loyal to his king, even if he was evil.

- Honored the king because he honored God.

- Was trusted by the king.

If your heart is like Daniel's, if you are willing to serve and give away what God has given you, then you will reach the mountain tops of your life wherever you go. On the mountain tops:

- God's Kingdom will come.

- Heaven will touch earth.

- The enemy's kingdom of darkness will fall.

- Nothing will be impossible.

- People's lives and places will change.

- Revival will happen!

- You will complete your royal mission.

Let the journey begin!

Time with Your King

This is going to be a very special time with your Dad. Begin by saying, "I love you, Dad."

Climb into His lap and just rest in His arms. Listen to what He says.

He will tell you again how much He loves you. You'll feel special. You'll feel rich.

Tell your Father how happy you are to be one of His children, one of His royal rulers.

Let Him know you want His Kingdom to come.

Tell Him you want to show His love and power to others wherever you go.

Ask God to show you the mountains—the different parts of your life.

He will show you what they are.

You will see your home, school, church, and where you hang out.

Open your heart. Let your Father show you what He has given you for your royal mission.

Thank Him for each one.

Thank your Guide and Friend, the Holy Spirit.

Ask the Father to touch your heart, your backpack. Ask Him for the heart of Daniel.

He will give you a heart to serve, honor, and help others even if they are evil right now.

God will touch their hearts as you show them His love.

Thank your heavenly Father for this special time.

Journal Time

1. Write about what your Father showed you and gave you.

2. What mountains of your life did you see?

3. Write down what you saw in your heart.

4. What is your heart, or backpack, like?

5. Is it like Daniel's?

6. Did God show you any people He wants you to serve and help? Write their names.

7. Do you feel as if you can climb to the top of your mountains?

Mission Objectives

As your Father shows you the mountains, the different areas of your life, begin to pray for Heaven to come.

God will show you what to release from Heaven. He will show you what to defeat and lock up on earth.

The Holy Spirit will lead you to people you can help and serve.

He will give you pictures and words about them. They will be words that will help them and make them feel loved.

They will feel that God is not angry at them.

They will feel God loves them, and that He is not far away.

Don't be shy. Let the Holy Spirit help you.

Write what happened when you told them the wonderful things that God said about them.

Be willing to give away what God has given you. Write about the miracles that happened when you prayed for people.

Write about how people are changing.

Write about how the mountains are changing in your life.

Be like Daniel and thank God for everything that happens.

ABOUT BILL JOHNSON

Bill Johnson is a fifth-generation pastor with a rich heritage in the Holy Spirit. Together Bill and his wife serve a growing number of churches that have partnered for revival. This leadership network has crossed denominational lines, building relationships that enable church leaders to walk successfully in both purity and power.

Bill and Brenda (Beni) Johnson are the senior pastors of Bethel Church, Redding, California. All three of their children and spouses are involved in full-time ministry. They also have nine wonderful grandchildren.

Printed in Great Britain
by Amazon.co.uk, Ltd.,
Marston Gate.